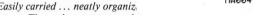

ALSO AVAILABLE IN THE COMPLEAT TRAVELER SERIES

☐ *Ferguson's* Europe by Eurail: *How to Tour Europe by Train*

☐ *Ferguson's* Britain by BritRail: *How to Tour Britain by Train*

☐ *Fistell's* America by Train: *How to Tour America by Rail*

☐ Bed & Breakfast America: *Great American Guest House Book*

☐ National & State Parks: *Lodges, Cabins, & Resorts*

☐ MacNeice: *National Sites, Monuments, and Battlefields*

☐ **Country Inns** & Historic Hotels of Great Britain

☐ **Country Inns** & Historic Hotels of Canada

☐ **Country Inns** & Historic Hotels of Ireland

☐ **Country** New England **Inns**

☐ **Country Inns** & Historic Hotels of the Middle Atlantic States

☐ **Country Inns** & Historic Hotels of the South

☐ **Country Inns** & Historic Hotels of the Midwest & Rocky Mts.

☐ **Country Inns** & Historic Hotels of California & the Northwest

☐ Guide to Country New England

☐ Guide to California & Pacific N.W.

☐ Guide to Texas and the Southwest

☐ *Scheer's* Guide to Virginia

☐ *Scheer's* Guide to North Carolina

☐ *Scheer's* Guide to Tennessee

☐ *Scheer's* Guide to Florida

If your local bookseller, gift shop, or country inn does not stock a particular title, ask them to order directly from Burt Franklin & Co., Inc., 235 East 44th Street, New York, 10017, U.S.A. Telephone orders are accepted from recognized retailers and credit-card holders. In the U.S.A., call, toll-free, 1-800-223-0766 during regular business hours. (In New York State, call 212-687-5250.)

Country Inns and Historic Hotels
of
Great Britain

Eileen and Eugene O'Reilly

BURT FRANKLIN & CO.

Published by
BURT FRANKLIN & COMPANY
235 East Forty-fourth Street
New York, New York 10017

SIXTH EDITION

Copyright © 1979, 1982, 1983,
1984, 1985, and 1986 by Burt Franklin & Co., Inc.

Library of Congress Cataloging in Publication Data

O'Reilly, Eileen.
Country inns and historic hotels of Great Britain.
(The Compleat traveler's companion)
Includes index.
1. Hotels, taverns, etc. — Great Britain — Directories.
I. O'Reilly, Eugene.   II. Title.
III. Series: Compleat traveler's companion.
TX910.G7073   1986   647′944101
ISBN 0–89102–325-9 (pbk.)

Cover Photo: Ye Olde Bell at Hurley

Manufactured in the United States of America

Published simultaneously in Canada by
FITZHENRY & WHITESIDE
195 Allstate Parkway
Markham, Ontario L3R 4T8

1 3 4 2

CONTENTS

*Abberley • Aldeburgh • Ambleside • Arundel • Aston Clinton
• Bainbridge • Bassenthwaite Lake • Bibury • Bishops Tachbrook
• Blanchland • Blawith • Blockley • Bolton-by-Bowland
• Bonchurch • Bosham • Bovey Tracey • Brampton
• Branscombe • Broadway • Burford • Burnsall
• Bury St Edmunds • Canterbury • Cartmel • Chagford
• Cheltenham • Chipping Campden • Climping • Constantine Bay
• Cornhill-on-Tweed • Coxwold • Crackington Haven
• Cranbrook • Crook • Crosby-on-Eden • Dedham • Diddlebury
• Dorchester-on-Thames • East Grinstead • Evershot • Frampton
• Giggleswick • Gittisham • Goudhurst • Grasmere
• Great Langdale • Greta Bridge • Grimsthorpe • Hawkhurst
• Henley-on-Thames • Horton-cum-Studley • Hovingham
• Huntsham • Hurley • Kilve • Kirkbymoorside • Lacock
• Lamorna • Lavenham • Ledbury • Lifton • Lincoln • London
• Long Melford • Ludlow • Lyndhurst • Malmesbury
• Mawnan Smith • Midhurst • Moreton-in-Marsh • Mousehole
• New Milton • Otterburn • Pooley Bridge • Poughill
• Rowsley • Rye • St. Austell • Shurdington • St. Columb Major
• Slaidburn • South Zeal • Southam • Stamford
• Stratford-upon-Avon • Sturminster Newton • Tetbury
• Thornbury • Upper Slaughter • Watermillock • Welland
• Wells • West Witton • Westonbirt • Weybourne
• Whitwell-on-the-Hill • Wilmcote • Windermere • Winsley
• Woodstock • York*

INTRODUCTION

To THOSE WHO DELIGHT in independent travel we offer this book and wish them happy journeys, sunny adventures, meetings with interesting strangers, and a warm welcome at the end of the day.

Enjoying a lodging is a highly subjective pleasure. We cannot tell you where to go; we can only tell you where we have been and why we liked it, hoping that you can choose from our descriptions those places that are right for you. Accommodations range from some of the most luxurious hotels in Britain to homespun, relatively inexpensive little inns, each with its own kind of appeal. When we travel we enjoy experiencing another time as well as another place, so all of these hotels are legacies of an earlier age, some of them incredibly old, others from the more recent past.

It was only after some hesitation that we decided to criticize a little here and there certain minor drawbacks, since it seemed not quite "nice" to find fault with some aspect of a pleasant place where the innkeeper was working hard to please. We ourselves, along with other members of our family, are owners of an inn, the Inn at Castle Hill in Newport, Rhode Island. We do not manage it—it is leased—but we are well aware of the hard work that is required to run an inn successfully. We were told by the author of a guide to American inns never to criticize—just recommend or leave out. But very few, if any, hotels are perfect. We have been disappointed with a lodging, glowingly described in some guidebook, that we might have enjoyed had there not been such a discrepancy between expectation and fact. An overrated place is a letdown, whereas the same place can be enjoyed (or avoided) when the drawbacks are expected.

In some good hotels you will find atmospheric public rooms but bedrooms that are not well decorated. We use the word "plain" to describe rooms that are clean and comfortable but decorated without style or charm. We have been pleased with every one of these lodgings, slept in some and eaten in others, and discussed them with other travelers recently returned from visits to them.

We do not name the almost four hundred hotels, usually well recommended, that we checked and found wanting. Some were so badly modernized, architecturally or decoratively, that we could only shudder and keep repeating, "What a pity!" Orange plastic and rock music in a historic inn are somehow not unlike a grandmother in a bikini. Other inns, though atmospheric, were musty. Even the most dedicated antiquarian finds little romantic about antique smells. Many of the inns were adequate but without charm, and at one otherwise lovely Cotswold manor the staff seemed to find the guests an unfortunate nuisance.

Although care has been taken to make sure our information is correct, there will inevitably be some changes after this book has gone to press — a hotel closed or sold, opening later or closing earlier in the season, an increase in price. Price categories listed in the text should be considered only as indications of the relative cost of the establishments. Rates should always be checked when making reservations.

We like to receive reports from our readers on their experiences with these hotels. You can write to us at Box 484R, Newport, Rhode Island, 02840. We would also welcome hearing about our readers' own favorites.

Bay Tree

TRAVEL TIPS

OUR EXPERIENCE INDICATES THAT it is best to have a reservation for the first night no matter how much of a vagabond you fancy yourself; to spend that night no more than 40 miles from the airport, preferably nearer, if you are renting a car there; and to reserve rooms ahead if you plan to stop over in a city. Driving and parking are too difficult to allow a search for a hotel room. If you arrive early in the day and don't like what you find, you can search further before registering. It may be worth it to you to change lodgings and lose a deposit. On the other hand, you may be more satisfied with what you have reserved once you have seen the alternatives.

The idea of driving through the countryside and stopping at some cozy little inn when the mood strikes has a fine romantic lilt to it, and that was the way we wanted to travel. We gradually learned that it was far more romantic to sleep in a four-poster in a famous smugglers' inn, where we had reserved in advance, than it was to spend the night in a commercial hotel because everything romantic was already taken.

We prefer to travel to Great Britain on British Airways. When we hear the distinctive British voices of the flight attendants, we feel that our British experience has already begun. We have found that we can reserve our car at a discount if we make arrangements through the airline at the time we book our flight; if we want, we can return that car at the airport in either Glasgow, Edinburgh, or Manchester without a drop-off penalty and take a British Airways shuttle that connects with our flight home from London.

To ensure an answer when you write abroad for a reservation, include an international reply coupon that you have purchased from your post office. Many hotels, especially small guest houses, cannot afford to pay postage to tell you, and perhaps dozens of others, that they are already full on the dates you require. We find that if we include a deposit in the form of a personal check, we are more likely to secure a reservation. If the lodging cannot take you, it will return the deposit. We make a few reservations ahead before we leave home if we especially want to stay in some hotels we know to be so highly recommended they are always booked well in advance. We leave nights open between reservations for flexibility and for the unexpected find that might be marvelous. We have learned to start looking for a lodging by 3 P.M. Sometimes we find a room in an inn we like on our first try. Sometimes we do not. Then we have time to drive on and seek another. The most unsatisfactory lodgings we've stayed in were the ones we checked in to after 5 P.M. By then the charmers are often full. After hearing three or four times that there is no room at the inn, the tendency is to settle for the first clean place that will take you. In season it is wise to have your hotel telephone ahead for a reservation in some recommended place. A popular hotel is more likely to accept an unsecured reservation from another hotel than from you, a stranger. Hotels expect to telephone for you. Don't wait until you are checking out to ask them to, however, as it can take hours for calls to go through. And be sure to telephone and cancel as early as possible if something keeps you from reaching that reserved room.

It has been said that no European takes a room without first inspecting it, while Americans ask for a room with a bath and take whatever they are assigned. If the hotel is full, you will obviously have no selection, but we suggest that you always ask upon arrival to see other rooms. We have often preferred a master bedroom in an old manor house, with the bath down the hall, to a more modern and more expensive small room with a private bath recently converted from servants' quarters. Two rooms sharing one bath may be more desirable than the two with private baths — excellent if you are traveling with another couple. You may also decide you don't like any of the rooms, and if you reach this decision by 3 P.M., the hotel will have time to rent the room again, and you can feel free to drive on to find lodging elsewhere.

One of the easiest ways to save money is to take a room without a private bath. As an innkeeper once said to me, "Most Americans think that taking a room without a private bath is positively *un-American*." Perhaps they have visions of standing in a hallway dressed in a bathrobe, toothbrush in hand, waiting in line to get into the bathroom. We have never seen, much less experienced, such a scene. There is usually a washbasin in a bedroom without a private bathroom, and there is almost always more than one hall bathroom. In Britain, unlike some countries in Continental Europe, hall bathrooms are not kept locked, and you do not have to make an appointment or pay to take a bath. Some of the most luxurious hotels in this guide have some rooms without private bath, and the difference in price can be up to £20 a night.

We suggest you plan to stay about 100 miles from your previous lodging. You will be on back roads that twist and turn — or if you aren't, you should be. Your actual mileage will be more, because you will detour to see historic and scenic spots along the way. You will take time to go into a museum, a garden, an ancient little church, a magnificent cathedral. If you feel like more driving after you have settled into an inn, there is nothing to prevent you from exploring the surrounding countryside.

We are told, "But I must see as much as possible. I may not get there again." What you will see will be more highways. Distances covered are not important, but quality of experience is. We find that a stay of about three days in each lodging is the most enjoyable way to go. It is delightful to return after a day of sightseeing to join other guests you have already met — to have the staff greet you by name and ask after your day's meandering. Also, many hotels give a reduced rate for a stay of two, three, or more days, usually on the modified American plan (MAP), which includes dinner. Always establish what plan you are taking before you register. If you decide after a day to move on, you can simply pay the one-day rate and leave. But if you register for the bed and breakfast rate and then decide to stay on, you cannot always get the reduced rate.

You will absorb the atmosphere of Britain far more by spending an occasional day out of your car, browsing in an antique store, having tea and scones in a little shop where the other seats are occupied by local housewives laden with string shopping bags, or eating lunch in the local pub, where it is easy to converse with the natives if you ask a few questions about the town's sights or history. Remember that in British pubs patrons are not seated separately. You find a seat at any table that has room. You walk to the bar to get your own drinks and pay for these as you receive them, not when you are through eating. Neither teetotalers nor unescorted ladies should hesitate to eat in pubs. We talked with an Australian couple at our hotel one evening who said their only problem was finding a place to get a light lunch. When we asked if they hadn't lunched in pubs, they said they didn't drink. We assured them that soft drinks are dispensed almost as frequently as alcoholic beverages at lunchtime in pubs.

Despite our love for back roads, we have to say that it is sometimes best to get on the superhighways. On our first trip we were determined not to use them. We would see the "real" Britain. Many trips later, we know that when we want to get around a city or go through an industrial area the superhighway is the only way to go. The alternative roads are the "real" Britain, all right. They are just as real as any road leading into an American city, clogged with traffic and lined with shopping malls, used-car lots, building complexes, and restaurants and nightclubs with neon signs. They are the kind of commercial enterprises necessary to any city but not what we go to Britain to see.

SOME THINGS TO
TAKE WITH YOU

Sectional road maps of Great Britain. We cannot emphasize too strongly how necessary we feel these to be. Every back road is drawn in, as are most small villages. These maps are hard to find in the United States. If you do not bring them with you, buy them as soon as you arrive. We like the Shell maps, divided into seven areas besides London. Most gas stations sell them, as well as some bookstores.

A single map of all Great Britain. The British Tourist Authority at 680 Fifth Avenue, New York, New York 10019, will send one free that has scenic areas marked. It will also send a London map.

We like to carry an atlas to Britain also. The index is helpful in finding small villages that may be hard to locate on even the area maps. You can buy one in Britain, ask your local bookstore to order one, or write to The British Travel Bookshop, 680 Fifth Avenue, New York, New York 10019. It might seem that with an atlas you won't need the individual maps. On the maps, however, it is easier to see several counties at once. With the atlas you must keep flipping pages, and there may be times when you want an overall picture of a larger area.

An *electrical converter set*, a small folding high-intensity *lamp*, and an *extension cord*. If you like to read in bed, don't count on a good reading light in every country inn. Sometimes all you will need is a 75-watt bulb to replace the 25-watt bulb you may find in the inn's bedside lamp. You must buy one when you get to Britain, as American bulbs do not fit British lamp sockets.

Other items we have found useful include a plastic bottle of detergent (you can buy one after you arrive), a travel clothesline with suction cups, inflatable plastic clothes hangers, a plastic cleaner's bag to place under dripping laundry (packed between folds of clothing in your suitcase it helps keep wrinkles away), a roll of large plastic bags (for enclosing damp laundry and many other uses), a sewing kit and a Buttoneer (for attaching buttons without sewing), a travel alarm clock, a small flashlight, eyeglass prescriptions.

HOW TO READ THE LISTINGS

Breaks   Special rates apply for a two- or three-day stay at certain times. The package includes meals and sometimes a tour, activity, or free use of some special facility.

Children free sharing   Children sharing a room with two adults are not charged except for meals taken.

Cocktail bar
Public bar   While some cocktail bars are for the use of the resident guests only, others also serve the public. In general, the atmosphere of a cocktail bar is more luxurious than that of a public bar. A public bar is heavily patronized by local people.

Credit cards   In Great Britain MasterCard is called Access and Visa is called Barclaycard.

Double room   When asking for a double room, specify whether you will accept a double bed, twin beds, or either. (We have been told, "No, we have no double room, only one with twin beds.")

Early and late snacks   Snacks are usually served just at lunchtime. Where we say, "early and late," they are served at suppertime also or, rarely, all afternoon and into the evening.

Fishing and shooting   Fishing and shooting are listed only under hotels that advise that gear can be rented or borrowed.

Golf   Golf is listed only under hotels that state that golf clubs can be rented or borrowed. If you have your own clubs, there is hardly a lodging that can't arrange for you to play golf on one of the more than 1,800 golf courses in Britain.

Ground-floor rooms Elevator	Though not necessarily suitable for guests dependent on wheelchairs, accommodations so labeled are desirable for those who do not want to climb stairs. Never ask for a room on the first floor if you want to be on the ground floor. In Britain, the first floor is the floor above the ground floor — what Americans call the second floor.
How to get there	If no detailed directions are given, the hotel will be easy to find in the center of the village. We do not give directions in London. (When driving into London, we have hired a taxi on the outskirts to lead us to our rental-car drop-off place. The taxi then takes us to our hotel.) When the hotel will meet guests at an airport or railway station, there will be a charge unless otherwise noted, and arrangements must be made with the hotel when reserving your room.
Hunting	The hotel will arrange for the guest to join a hunt.
Luncheon	Luncheon is a sit-down meal served in a dining room.
Off-season rates	Off-season rates vary among hotels, with some raising rates at Easter, others as late as July. Rates could be reduced anytime from September to January.
Rates	Prices can go out of date soon after a guide is published. We note under the description of each lodging a comparative price rating so the reader can know how it compares in price to all others in the guide. Some hotels will fall into two categories because some of their rooms are more expensive than others. These prices are for two people in the 1985 high season and include breakfast (usually a full breakfast but in a few cases a Continental breakfast), service, and tax. *Actual rates are listed in the index.*

very inexpensive	up to £27
inexpensive	£28 to £42
moderate	£43 to £65
expensive	£66 to £80
very expensive	more than £80

Reduction	A reduction is made for a stay of two or three days all year, usually MAP (Modified American Plan), which includes dinner. Always establish the rate and plan before registering.
Restaurant service	All meals listed under each entry are served to the general public, not just to house guests. All lodgings recommended in this book serve breakfast to house guests. All serve dinner to house guests unless noted otherwise in the write-up of that lodging. In addition, many serve luncheon, snacks, or tea to house guests but not to the general public. All lodgings in this guide serve licensed beverages to both restaurant and house guests unless noted otherwise in the write-up.

The listings do not necessarily apply on Sunday. Some hotels serve only a large traditional dinner Sunday at midday. They may not be open on Sunday evening, or they may serve a cold buffet, sometimes only to house guests. Few serve snacks or tea on Sunday.

Snacks	A snack is a light meal, sometimes just bread and cheese (called a ploughman's lunch), sometimes sandwiches, hot soup, meat pies, and occasionally a buffet from which you choose and pay for only what you want. It is usually served in a tavern or pub but sometimes on a tray in a lounge and often, in good weather, outside. (Our first day in England we began to feel rejected when three pubs told us they could not give us lunch, and at the third one there were sandwiches made up at the bar. "Can't we buy some of those?" we asked. "Oh, *snacks*! Of course, dear, you can have *snacks*. We don't have *lunch*. But I could cook you some nice ham and eggs if you'd like." Unless you want a formal meal served in a dining room, don't ask for lunch.)
Supper	Supper is a light dinner, called high tea in Britain, usually served before the dinner hour or, in a few hotels, in a second dining room that serves only light meals.
[T]	The hotel will pay a travel agent a commission on rooms. The percentage varies among hotels.

Tea	Afternoon tea includes such items as scones, tea sandwiches, or cake — not just a commercially baked cookie (which is called a biscuit).
Tea-making	The bedroom is equipped with facilities to make tea and coffee (electric kettle, cups, spoons, tea bags, instant coffee, sugar and creamer).
Telephone	The number in parentheses is the STD, or area, code. Many places in Great Britain can be dialed direct from America. For instructions ask the operator or dial (800) 874-4000.
U.S. Agents	Some British hotels are represented by the following American agents. You or your travel agent may call these for reservations for the hotels that list an American agent.

Abercrombie and Kent International, Inc. (800) 323-3602; in Illinois, (312) 954-2944

Best Western (800) 528-1234; in Arizona, (800) 352-1222; in Phoenix, 954-7600

Consort Hotels (800) 223-6764; in New York State, (800) 522-5568; in New York City, (212) 758-4375

David Mitchell & Company, Inc. (212) 696-1323

Josephine Barr (800) 323-5463; in Illinois, (312) 251-4110

Ray Morrow Associates (800) 243-9420; in Connecticut, (203) 438-3793 collect

Romantik Hotels (800) 826-0015; in Washington, (206) 885-5805

Scott Calder (800) 223-5581; in New York State, (212) 535-9530 collect

THF (Trust Houses Forte) (800) 223-5672; in New York City, (212) 541-4400

With bath	Specify if a private bathroom with tub *or* shower is acceptable. (We have been told, "No, we have no room with a private bath, only one with a shower.") Occasionally, a private bathroom must be reached through a public hall. If it is important for you to have a private bathroom opening directly into your bedroom, specify a bathroom *en suite*.

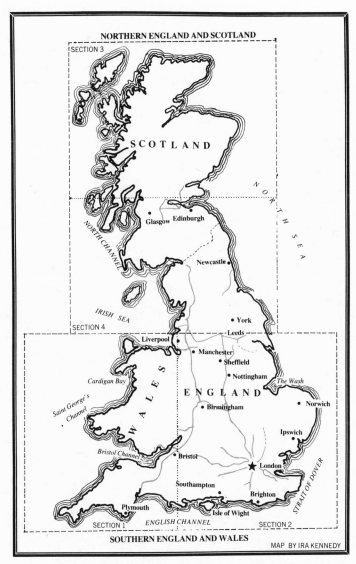

NORTHERN ENGLAND AND SCOTLAND

SECTION 3

SCOTLAND

NORTH SEA

NORTH CHANNEL

Glasgow • Edinburgh

Newcastle

IRISH SEA

York

SECTION 4

Leeds

Liverpool

Manchester

Sheffield

Nottingham

Cardigan Bay

WALES

ENGLAND

The Wash

Saint George's Channel

Birmingham

Norwich

Bristol Channel

Bristol

Ipswich

London

Southampton

Brighton

STRAIT OF DOVER

Plymouth

Isle of Wight

SECTION 1

ENGLISH CHANNEL

SECTION 2

SOUTHERN ENGLAND AND WALES

MAP BY IRA KENNEDY

MAP / 15

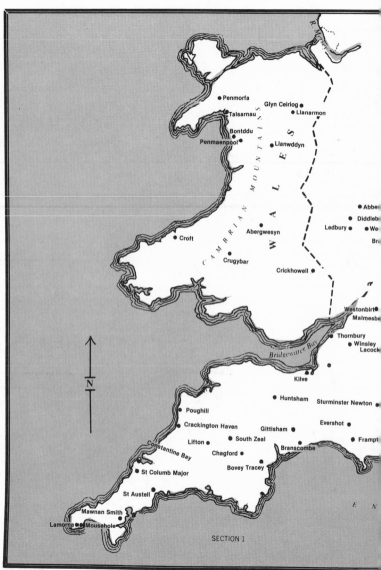

SECTION 1

NORTH SEA

Rowsley

● Lincoln

● Grimsthorpe

Weybourne ●

E   N   G   L   A   N   D

Stamford ●

Bishops Tachbrook
        ●   ● Southam
Wilmcote
● Stratford-upon-Avon
ipping Campden
ockley
● Moreton-in-March

● Upper Slaughter
        ● Woodstock   Aston Clinton
ington ● Horton-cum-Studley   ●
● Burford
ury
        ● Dorchester-on-Thames

Henley-on-Thames ●   ● Hurley

● Bury St Edmunds

Lavenham ●
Long Melford ●

● Dedham

London
★

R. Thames

Canterbury ●

Goudhurst ●   ● Cranbrook
        ● East Grinstead
                ● Hawkhurst

Rye ●

Midhurst ●
        ● Arundel
●● Bosham
Isle of
Wight
● Bonchurst

Climping

ISH   CHANNEL

SOUTHERN ENGLAND AND WALES

SECTION 2

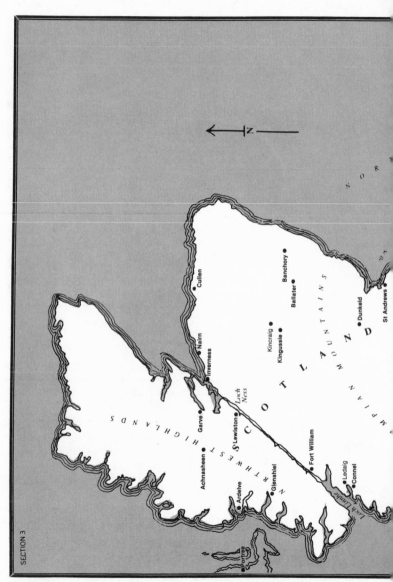

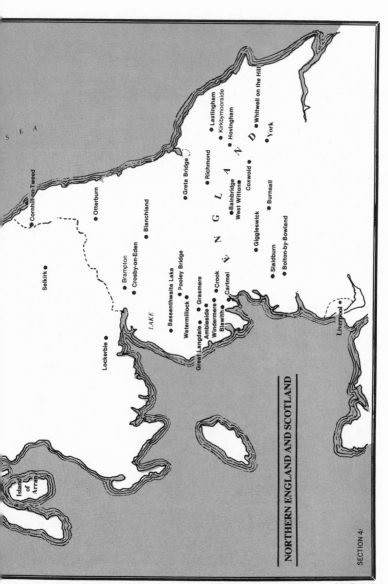

NORTHERN ENGLAND AND SCOTLAND

SECTION 4:

Highland

Grampion

SCOTLAND

Tayside

Central   Fife

Lothian

Strathclyde

Borders

Northumbria

Lake
District

Lancashire

Yorkshire

North
West

The Marches

West
Midlands

East Midlands

*Shakespeare
Country*

W A L E S

Cotswolds

East Anglia

Thames and
Chilterns

★ London

Southern
England

South East England

West Country

Isle of Wight

ENGLAND

LIST OF TOWNS BY REGION

Readers interested in visiting a particular region will find it listed below with the names of its towns in alphabetical order as they appear in the text.

The Cotswolds and Shakespeare Country: Bibury, Bishops Tachbrook, Blockley, Broadway, Burford, Chipping Campden, Moreton-in-Marsh, Shurdington, Southam, Stratford-upon-Avon, Tetbury, Upper Slaughter, Westonbirt, Wilmcote

East Anglia: Aldeburgh, Bury St Edmunds, Dedham, Lavenham, Long Melford, Weybourne

The East Midlands: Grimsthorpe, Lincoln, Rowsley, Stamford

The Lake District: Ambleside, Bassenthwaite Lake, Blawith, Brampton, Cartmel, Crook, Crosby-on-Eden, Grasmere, Great Langdales, Pooley Bridge, Watermillock, Windermere

Lancashire: Bolton-by-Bowland, Slaidburn

The Marches: Abberley, Diddlebury, Ledbury, Ludlow, Welland

Northumbria: Blanchland, Cornhill-on-Tweed, Otterburn,

South East England: Canterbury, Cranbrook, East Grinstead, Goudhurst, Hawkhurst, Rye

Southern England: Arundel, Bonchurch, Bosham, Climping, Lyndhurst, Midhurst, New Milton

Thames and Chilterns: Aston Clinton, Dorchester-on-Thames, Henley-on-Thames, Horton-cum-Studley, Hurley, London, Wendover, Woodstock

The West Country: Bovey Tracey, Branscombe, Chagford, Constantine Bay, Crackington Haven, Evershot, Frampton, Gittisham, Huntsham, Kilve, Lacock, Lamorna, Lifton, Malmesbury, Mawnan Smith, Mousehole, Poughill, St Austell, St Columb Major, St Mawes, South Zeal, Sturminster Newton, Thornbury, Wells, Winsley

Yorkshire: Bainbridge, Burnsall, Coxwold, Giggleswick, Greta Bridge, Hovingham, Kirkbymoorside, West Witton, Whitwell-on-the-Hill, York

ELMS

A thing of beauty is a joy forever.

John Keats

This beautiful building, constructed in 1710 in the reign of Queen Anne and designed by a pupil of the renowned Sir Christopher Wren, is a building of special architectural interest. It looks very grand and formal, but a warm country welcome awaits the traveler.

When we arrived at teatime, a wood fire burned gently. The high-ceilinged drawing room held books and fresh flowers. One could imagine that Edith Wharton and Henry James were among the guests sitting on the velvet chairs and tufted sofas.

A wide, thickly carpeted oak staircase leads to bedrooms with spectacular views. The Library Bar, which retains its fine old mahogany bookcases, in warm weather opens onto the adjacent terrace overlooking the 12 acres of parkland, formal gardens, and putting green. All the rooms contain handsome paintings and interesting oddments, such as a mahogany knife box converted to a depository for outgoing mail. Candlelight dinners in the Regency dining room have been recommended in British food guides.

Yesterday lingers gracefully at the Elms, a good choice for those for whom travel means staying in places they aren't likely to forget.

Proprietor: Ms. Mooney. *Recreational facilities:* Tennis and putting green at the hotel. *Other facilities:* 2 drawing rooms, lounge, cocktail bar, garden, laundry service. *Rooms:* 20 with bath, TV, and telephone; suites. Suitable for wheelchair guests. Weekend breaks; Christmas program. No children under 3. Moderate to expensive. *Restaurant service:* Luncheon, dinner. *Credit cards:* All. *How to get there:* Abberley is about 10 miles northwest of Worcester. Leave Route M5 at exit 7. The Elms is on Route A443.

Telephone: (029 921) 666. *Agent in the United States:* Scott Calder.   [T]

UPLANDS HOTEL

> I belong at home in Aldeburgh . . . all the music I write comes from it.
>
> *Benjamin Britten*

This unpretentious, pleasant hotel was the childhood home of Elizabeth Garrett Anderson, Britain's first woman doctor. The living rooms are like those of a private house, with magazines and books about. At the informal bar, one day, some jolly Englishmen, down for golf, each wanted to buy the Americans an after-dinner drink.

The food in the attractive dining room, which is larger and more formal than the rest of the rooms of the hotel, with many area patrons, was delicious. We much prefer the bedrooms in the main house, though only one has a private bath, to the small, motel-like rooms built in the garden.

Several operas by Benjamin Britten, eminent composer and Aldeburgh native, were performed for the first time at the famous Aldeburgh Festival, held each June. Boats to sail, row, canoe, or punt can be hired at a lake safe for children, as can sailboats on the River Alde, with instruction if desired.

Shops line the streets paralleling the sea at this small seaside resort, where fishing boats go out from the beach. We did not care for any of the beachfront hotels but were very happy at Uplands.

Proprietors: Robert, Patricia, and Nicola Tidder. *Recreational facilities:* Swimming and tennis a short walk away; golf a short drive away. *Other facilities:* Lounge, TV lounge, sun parlor, cocktail bar, garden. *Rooms:* 20, 8 with bath, some with TV. Ground-floor rooms. Winter breaks; Christmas program. Inexpensive to moderate. *Restaurant service:* Dinner. *Credit cards:* Amex, Master, Visa. *How to get there:* Aldeburgh is on the Suffolk coast. The hotel is on Victoria Road (Route 1094) at the edge of town. *Telephone:* (072 885) 2420.

NAB COTTAGE

> We passed The Nab, in which De Quincey formerly lived,
> and where Hartley Coleridge lived and died. It is a small,
> buff-tinted, plastered stone cottage, I should think of a
> very humble class originally; but it now looks as if per-
> sons of taste might sometime or other have set down in it,
> and caused flowers to spring up about it.
>
> *Nathaniel Hawthorne,* 1854

Nab Cottage, crowded with literary associations, brings memories of the
poets who made the Lake District so famous. It was the farm home of the
girl Thomas De Quincey married after their child was born. The marriage
was a happy one, although De Quincey was dropped by his friends the
Wordsworths, partly for marrying a "low-class woman." Some years
afterward he lived in the house with his family. When they moved away,
Wordsworth arranged a lease on it for Hartley Coleridge, beloved
schoolmaster in the village, the talented but ill-fated son of Samuel

Taylor Coleridge and nephew of Robert Southey. Then the Wordsworth family visited Nab Cottage frequently.

The house is across the road from Rydal Lake, where Wordsworth liked to ice-skate. A desk reputed to have belonged to Coleridge is among the furnishings at Nab Cottage, and all its bedrooms hold some old pieces. A home-cooked dinner is offered, with wine but no other spirits available. Among the guests who gather for evening tea before a coal fire in the lounge are many who return year after year, some revisiting the house where they stayed as children. Professors of literature are particularly drawn to the inn.

If you take the short walk to Rydal Mount, Wordsworth's last home and now a museum, you can almost see the poet striding along the road, his faithful sister Dorothy by his side, sometimes speaking aloud as he tries out a line of verse evolving in his head. At Rydal Mount you can picture him seated there surrounded by the women who waited on him so devotedly: sister, wife, daughter, sister-in-law. The peace and simplicity of the England of the poets cling to Nab Cottage and its surroundings.

Proprietor: Jean Melling. *Closed:* December through February. *Recreational facilities:* Indoor pool, lake swimming, tennis, squash, riding, boat rental, and boat trips a short drive away. *Facilities for children:* Baby-sitting and -listening. *Other facilities:* Lounge, TV lounge, garden. *Rooms:* 7 sharing baths. Reduction for children sharing (under 2 free). Very inexpensive. *How to get there:* Nab Cottage is on Route A591 between Grasmere and Ambleside. *Telephone:* (096 65) 311.

ROTHAY MANOR

Our road lay through Ambleside, which is certainly a very pretty town, and looks cheerfully in a sunny day.
Nathaniel Hawthorne, 1854

This refined Regency house, relaxed and friendly with its flower-laden atmosphere, is filled with paintings and prints, antiques that range from carved Jacobean mirrors to Victorian chairs, and those tipsy, elaborate lampshades that we love in Europe and that would look hilarious if we took them back home. Log fires are lighted on chilly days. Outside the sunny bay windows, white garden furniture looks irresistible beside flower beds and a croquet lawn under imposing old trees.

A winter program provides special dinners on Wednesdays and Fridays. Cooking and wines from various regions of France are featured, along with wine tastings and demonstrations of such crafts as furniture restoration using antique tools and glass engraving. In mid-December there is an evening of nostalgia when guests are welcomed with steaming drinks before listening to "Charles Dickens" read passages from his latest works. Then all sit to a dinner of roast Michaelmas goose and plum pudding, after which the young at heart play Victorian games like blind man's bluff and forfeits. For those who don't like to move around every day, this well-run hotel would be a delightful base from which to explore England's Lake District.

Proprietors: Bronwen Nixon and family. *Closed:* Early January to mid-February. *Recreational facilities:* Lake and river swimming and tennis a short walk away; coarse and trout fishing, riding, hunting, squash, and lake steamer a short drive away. *Facilities for children:* Children's supper. *Other facilities:* Drawing room, lounge, cocktail bar, garden. *Rooms:* 14 with bath, TV, telephone; 2 suites. Suitable for wheelchair guests. Off-season rates; breaks; 4-day Christmas program; 3-day New Year's program. Minimum two nights on weekends. Expensive. *Restaurant service:* Luncheon, tea, dinner. *Credit cards:* Amex, Diners, Master, Visa. *How to get there:* From Ambleside, at the northern tip of Lake Windermere, find Rothay Manor on the road marked "to Coniston." *Telephone:* (0966) 33605. *Agent in the United States:* Josephine Barr.

NORFOLK ARMS

> As they reach the foot of the hill, the guard commences a
> solo on his bugle, to give notice to the innkeeper to have
> the coach dinner on the table.
>
> *Robert Surtees,* 1831

Great was the glamour of the coaching age. On the steep High Street
rising from the River Arun, the Norfolk Arms once knew the music of
the guard's horn as the coach swept under the archway into the stable
yard.

The centuries have been kind to the Norfolk Arms. Some of the bedrooms contain four-posters, and the main hall is enhanced by many
antiques.

The hotel is somewhat impersonal, but Arundel is one of the loveliest
old towns in southern England. Its ancient buildings cluster beneath the
towers of majestic, historic Arundel Castle, ancestral home of the dukes
of Norfolk. No family in English history has a more tumultuous past
than the enormously wealthy Norfolks, whose lives have been entwined
with those of royalty through centuries of ancient plots and intrigues.
The castle has withstood siege three times. Beside it is a Roman Catholic
cathedral, for the Norfolks were one of the few titled families that held to
the old religion. You may go through the castle and its park, and you'll
enjoy the fine antique shops along the High Street.

Manager: David Horridge. *Recreational facilities:* Ocean swimming,
tennis, riding, golf, and boat rental a short drive away. *Facilities for children:* Children's supper. *Other facilities:* Lounge, cocktail bar. *Rooms:*
34, 32 with bath, all with TV, telephone, and tea-making. Suitable for
wheelchair guests. 2-day reduction; free for children under 15 sharing.
Inexpensive to moderate. *Restaurant service:* Luncheon, early and late
snacks, dinner. *Credit cards:* Amex, Diners, Master, Visa. *How to get
there:* Guests can be met at the Arundel railway station. *Telephone:*
(0903) 882101.   [T]

Aston Clinton, Buckinghamshire

BELL INN

> Alas! Alas! Where is it gone,
> That coach with its four bright bays?
> Alas! Alas! Where is it gone
> That spicey team of greys?
>
> *C. Birch Reynardson,* 1875

There are no coaches and horses outside the Bell today; you are much more likely to see a helicopter hovering among the trees, ready to land a guest. An officially listed historic building, once part of the estate of the Duke of Buckingham and known as an inn since at least 1650, the Bell has been developed into one of the most prestigious hostelries in Britain.

In 1939, it was bought by Gerard Harris, a lawyer by profession but a gourmet and restaurateur by inclination, a man "passionately interested in food and wine." It is now run by the Harris family and improving all the time, if that is possible. While there are always traditional British dishes—poached Scotch salmon, tipsy cake—and game in season, such as pheasant, wild duck, hare, venison, and partridge, fine French cooking predominates. It was a favorite of Evelyn Waugh's. The dining room draws discerning Londoners, so make a dinner reservation when you reserve your room.

Antique furnishings have been chosen as for a private house. Fourteen of the rooms are in converted stables and malt houses around a cobbled courtyard. Some have doors opening onto a garden, and each has fresh-flower arrangements, bath salts, a bathroom scale, those luxurious terry robes sometimes found in expensive European hotels, and a refrigerator stocked with drinks.

The inn is on a busy road in a fairly built-up area close to London, not far from Heathrow, and would be a grand place for a bang-up splurge your last night.

Proprietor: Michael Harris. *Rooms:* 21 with bath, TV, and telephone. Suitable for wheelchair guests. Discounts for children under 16 sharing. Expensive. *Restaurant service:* Luncheon, snacks, dinner. *Credit cards:* Master, Visa. *How to get there:* The inn is on Route A41, 4 miles east of Aylesbury. *Telephone:* (0296) 630252. *Agent in the United States:* David Mitchell.

[T]

ROSE AND CROWN

> The green tracks that wander everywhere over the flanks of the Pennines . . . seem to beg for people to walk over them, and this is one of the most rewarding experiences I know.
>
> *James Herriot,* 1979

In the midst of the Yorkshire that James Herriot describes in his popular books, the Rose and Crown faces the green in a lovely little moorland village. On that green three blasts have been blown on an ox horn every evening for more than five hundred years, to guide to shelter travelers lost in the forest of Wensleydale. The custom continues although the forests are gone. Bainbridge was a village even in Roman times, and the inn dates from 1445.

A collection of antiques enhances the inn's attractiveness. Residents of the area join hotel guests for special dinners and dances, with everyone soon on first-name terms. The inn's two single rooms are just half the price of the doubles.

The surrounding countryside is Yorkshire Dales National Park, designated to be left unspoiled now and for generations to come. In a hotel van, with a picnic lunch packed by the inn, local people guide guests on tours of some of the wildest fells in Yorkshire. We suggest you ask to go over the high Buttertubs Pass into Swaledale and through villages with such amusing names as Crackpot and Blubberhouses.

Proprietor: Penny Thorpe. *Recreational facilities:* River and lake swimming and riding a short drive away. *Other facilities:* 2 cocktail bars, public bar, garden. *Rooms:* 13, 6 with bath, all with TV and tea-making. Winter breaks; Christmas program. Inexpensive. *Restaurant service:* Snacks, dinner. *Credit cards:* Master, Visa. *How to get there:* Bainbridge is on Route A684 west of Leyburn. *Telephone:* (0969) 50225.

PHEASANT INN

D'ye ken John Peel with his coat so gay?
D'ye ken John Peel at the break of day?
D'ye ken John Peel when he's far far away
With his hounds and his horn in the morning?

John Graves, 1828

For pure charm, the Pheasant is a winner. The time-blackened beams and white plaster walls of this sixteenth-century inn give great character to rooms filled with groupings of chintz-covered chairs. Everything is bright and cheerful. Walls are decked with guns, sporting prints, blue and white china, and oil paintings. Welcoming fires and a "taste of England" menu are other attractions.

Local people like the original bar, where real ale is on tap. Electric blankets and full central heating keep visitors warm and comfortable all winter. To top it all, the price is right. The Pheasant Inn was a hangout for the legendary John Peel. The type of fox hunting for which he was famous — on foot, not horseback — starts in front of the inn. If you can't stay, stop in for afternoon tea, in the garden in good weather.

Manager: William Barrington-Wilson. *Closed:* Christmas. *Recreational facilities:* Lake swimming a short walk away; riding, hunting, boat rental, and boat trips a short drive away. *Other facilities:* 3 lounges, public bar, garden. *Rooms:* 20, 12 with bath. Suitable for wheelchair guests. 3-day reduction; 2-day breaks; reduction for children sharing. Moderate. *Restaurant service:* Luncheon, snacks, tea, dinner (no smoking). *How to get there:* The inn is on Route A66 at the head of Bassenthwaite Lake between Keswick and Cockermouth. *Telephone:* (059 681) 234.

Bibury, Gloucestershire

BIBURY COURT

> We procured the key of the church—a key the size of
> Dover Castle—and admired it as lightsome, and well-
> glazed.
>
> *John Byng,* 1794

A door in the wall of Bibury Court's garden leads into the churchyard of
a Saxon church admired by John Byng during his visit long ago to beautiful Bibury. This great house was built in 1633 by Sir Thomas Sackville,
illegitimate son of the first earl of Dorset and a "Knight and gentleman-
usher in dailie waiting on the King." Its spacious rooms are furnished in
the styles of different periods, from bedrooms with Jacobean oak four-
posters to the cocktail lounge decorated in the 1920s in Art Nouveau
style. A spirit of jollity prevails in a bar in the coach house where local
people congregate. Tea is served in the garden in summer.

If the ghost of Charles II, said to have been a visitor at Bibury Court,
wanders through the corridors, is he astonished at today's world, where
anyone with the price of a night's lodging can slumber in chambers once
reserved for nobles? Would the easygoing, affable Charles approve? You
will. You can't help but feel welcome here.

Proprietor: James Collier. *Closed:* Christmas. *Special facilities:*
Lounge, TV lounge, cocktail bar, public bar, garden. *Rooms:* 14 with
bath. Inexpensive. *Restaurant service:* Snacks, dinner. *Credit cards:*
Amex, Diners, Master, Visa. *How to get there:* Guests can be met at
Heathrow Airport or at the Kemble railway station. Bibury is on Route
A433 between Cirencester and Burford. *Telephone:* (028 574) 337.   [T]

Bishops Tachbrook, Warwickshire

MALLORY COURT

> For sure so fair a place was never seen
> Of all that ever charm's romantic eye.
>
> *John Keats,* 1818

This superb country house, set in 10 acres of cultivated gardens and velvet lawns, is a haven of peace and beauty. It was built early in this century, and much of the original furniture remains. What has since been added is in keeping with its luxurious setting.

A warm country-house atmosphere prevails. Guests relax on big sofas by an open log fire where afternoon tea or drinks are served. Bedrooms are splendidly comfortable, with little extras such as hair dryers and a selection of books.

The oak-paneled dining room serves classic French cuisine that has earned a star from Michelin. You might choose filet mignon topped with foie gras, truffles, and Madeira sauce, or calf's liver with wine, cream, and mustard sauce. The wine list is extensive. Fine china, silver, and crystal enhance the flawless service.

In any contest to choose England's best country-house hotels, Mallory Court would receive high marks.

Proprietors: Jeremy Mort and Alan Holland. *Closed:* December 26 – January 2. *Recreational facilities:* Outdoor pool and squash at the hotel; golf and riding nearby. *Other facilities:* Drawing room, garden, laundry-valet service. *Rooms:* 8 with bath, telephone, and TV; 1 suite. Not suitable for children under 14. Expensive to very expensive. *Restaurant service:* Luncheon and dinner. *Credit cards:* Amex, Master, Visa. *How to get there:* From Bishops Tachbrook, take Route A452 toward Leamington Spa, which is 2 miles away. Turn right onto Harbury Lane. Mallory Court is on the right. *Telephone:* (0926) 30214. *Agent in the United States:* David Mitchell. [T]

LORD CREWE ARMS

> On a sudden in the midst of men and day,
> And while I walk'd and talk'd as heretofore,
> I seem'd to move among a world of ghosts,
> And feel myself the shadow of a dream.
>
> *Alfred, Lord Tennyson*

If walls could talk, the yard-thick walls of the Lord Crewe Arms could tell swashbuckling tales of its turbulent past. It was part of an eleventh-century abbey, home of the White Monks until their massacre by raiders from the north. Centuries later, Tom Forster, a leading figure in the Jacobite rebellion, was hidden in the priest's hiding hole by his sister, Dorothy. On your way to today's Crypt Bar, through stone-flagged rooms and narrow passages, you will walk by this hiding hole in a vast chimney. History comes alive as you gaze into it and ponder the lives of the desperate fugitives who hid there. Dorothy haunts the hotel to this day.

On the cobbled market square of this village set amid heather-covered moors, the local hunt meets before the door of the hotel. A coal fire in a massive stone fireplace, with inglenook, greets the entering guest. Furnished with antiques from many periods, the Lord Crewe Arms is a fine place for history buffs who like to experience their history in comfort.

If you don't stay overnight, try to come by for morning coffee, afternoon tea, or a snack lunch served in the garden. Few inns have quite the ancient atmosphere of the Lord Crewe Arms.

Proprietor: Ermes Oretti. *Recreational facilities:* Sailboat rental a short drive away. *Facilities for children:* Baby-listening; children's meals. *Other facilities:* TV lounge, cocktail bar, public bar, garden. *Rooms:* 15 with bath and telephone. Off-season rates; children under 13 free sharing, reduction if in separate room. Moderate. *Restaurant service:* Early and late snacks, tea, dinner. *Credit cards:* Amex, Diners, Master, Visa. *How to get there:* Blanchland is 6 miles from Route A68 on the road to Stanhope. Guests can be met at the Hexham or Consett railway station. *Telephone:* (043 475) 251.   [T]

Blawith, Cumbria

APPLETREE HOLME FARM

This little unsuspected Paradise where all is peace.
                                                        Thomas Gray, 1757

One of the smallest gems in Britain is this lodging of extraordinary enchantment. Roy and Shirley Carlsen, having developed their last hotel into one of the most successful country houses in Britain, chose to exchange it for a farmhouse way out on the fells. They enjoy entertaining guests, which is why they entered the hotel business, but as their enterprise grew they found they had little time to spend with visitors. "We love being back to doing everything ourselves," said Shirley. "The nicest kind of people stay at small guest houses, and here we have time to talk to them."

The exterior of the simple farmhouse gives no hint of the luxury and taste within — antiques, oak timbers, beautiful ornaments, big open fires, a wall of books, pictures and flowers everywhere. One bedroom is in a separate cottage called Down House, next to the main house, with an outstanding view, a private patio, and one of the most glamorous bathrooms you are ever likely to come across. Another glamorous bathroom in the main house, with a double bubble bath, was such an unexpected find that it caused us to laugh with delight. Shirley chuckled as she watched us. "We don't warn anyone," she told us, "It's such fun to see their surprise."

All bookings accepted include dinner, and the cooking is as special as the house. Whenever possible they serve food produced on their own or neighboring farms. They bake their own bread and personally select meat, fish, and game. Besides the house guests, they'll serve only one party of up to six dinner guests. If you can manage it, plan to stay here for a week; just think how welcome those fires would feel in autumn after a hike across the fells.

Proprietors: Roy and Shirley Carlsen. *Closed:* Christmas through January 1. *Recreational facilities:* Lake swimming, riding, and rough shooting a short walk away; hunting, ocean swimming, game, coarse and sea fishing, boat rental, and boat trips a short drive away. *Other facilities:* Lounge, TV lounge, garden. *Rooms:* 4 with bath and tea-making. 2-night minimum advance reservation. Discount for children sharing. Inexpensive to moderate. *Restaurant service:* Dinner by reservation. *How to get there:* In Blawith, which is on Route A5084 just south of Coniston Water (a large lake), turn into a lane directly opposite the Saint John Baptist Church. After almost half a mile, take the first right. Follow this lane to the first left, where the farm is signposted. If you have any problem finding the farm, ask directions at the post office in Blawith. Guests can be met at the Ulverston railway station. *Telephone:* (022 985) 618.

Blockley, Gloucestershire

LOWER BROOK HOUSE

> Every antique farm house and moss-grown cottage is a
> picture.
> *Washington Irving*

This is the sort of place Washington Irving described, now a cozy hotel in a lovely village off the main path of the tourist throngs. When we

stopped in one morning, there was a fire burning gently in a vast inglenook fireplace bearing the date 1655; beside it was an enormous foot-operated bellows. The rooms were redolent of home-baked bread fresh from the oven. The proprietor, Ewan Wright, supervises the cooking and cares about the quality of the food served in the flagstoned dining room.

The whole of this small inn shines with loving care. Bowls of nuts, with nutcrackers handy, are placed casually on tables in the living room and lounge. Black beams are imbedded in the white plaster walls, decked with hunting horns of copper and brass. The small, newly furnished bedrooms all have views over the garden, and the recently installed bathrooms are excellent. On the third floor you'll slumber under ancient beams, but the bedrooms on the second are a bit larger. In summer, sip your drink beside a murmuring brook in the terraced garden of this happy blend of old and new.

Proprietor: Ewan Wright. *Closed:* Last 2 weeks in January. *Recreational facilities:* Riding, hunting, squash, and golf a short drive away. *Other facilities:* Lounge, cocktail bar, living room, garden. *Rooms:* 8 with bath; TV available. 3-day reduction; winter breaks. No children under 5. Moderate. *Restaurant service:* Luncheon, tea, dinner. *Credit cards:* Master, Visa. *How to get there:* Blockley is on Route B4479, which runs from A44 between Moreton-in-Marsh and Broadway. *Telephone:* (0386) 700286.

HARROP FOLD FARM

> Have you become a farmer? Is it not pleasanter than to be shut up within 4 walls and delving eternally with a pen? . . . If you are half as much delighted with the farm as I am, you bless your stars.
>
> *Thomas Jefferson*

Homespun friendliness is the rule at this seventeenth-century Lancashire Longhouse that has been featured as a farm guest house on the BBC and in *Lancashire Life* magazine. Many antiques are used in furnishings and accessories, but there are modern touches too. A tiny cattle barn called the Saetr, an old Norse word, was converted into two bedrooms, each with bathroom, and is decorated in Scandinavian style.

Very special farmhouse cooking at Harrop Fold emphasizes traditional English country recipes made with local produce. Dinner begins with soup—pea and ham, asparagus, cream of nettle—and continues with an appetizer, main course, dessert, cheese, and fruit, followed by coffee and mints in the lounge. Entrées might include roast turkey, crown roast of lamb, duckling with sage and onion stuffing, or game in season. There is a selection of sweets from the buffet: perhaps apple pie, bilberry tart, and syllabub trifle.

Breakfast prepares you for a day spent walking the fells (a telephone call will bring someone to pick you up if you get too tired to hike back). A buffet of fruits, juices, and cereals is followed by bacon, eggs, sausage, tomatoes, mushrooms, toast, croissants, honey, and homemade marmalade. The Woods have put together a booklet for less energetic types to guide them to Yorkshire dales or Cumbrian lakes and to antique shops, craftsmen, auctions, art galleries, and pubs.

Proprietors: Peter and Victoria Wood. *Recreational facilities:* Riding, hunting, tennis, squash, and indoor pool a short drive away. *Other facilities:* Lounge, TV lounge, cocktail bar, garden. *Rooms:* 7 with bath, TV and tea-making. Suitable for wheelchair guests. 2-day reduction. 4-day Christmas program. Not suitable for children. Inexpensive. *How to get there:* Do not go into the village of Bolton-by-Bowland. Find Harrop Fold signposted on the road between Grindleton and Slaidburn, somewhat nearer Grindleton. *Telephone:* (02007) 600.

Bonchurch, Isle of Wight

PEACOCK VANE

> Bonchurch is simply delicious and indeed in a manner quite absurd. It is like a model village in imitative substances, kept in a big glass case; the turf might be green velvet and the foliage of cut paper.
>
> *Henry James,* 1872

The Wolfendens have offered a welcome at Peacock Vane for more than a quarter of a century. In this Regency house, guests make their own drinks on top of the grand piano in the drawing room, which serves as a bar, with payment on the honor system. There is friendly fireside chatter as guests mingle cordially. The bedrooms are furnished with antiques and patchwork, some with four-posters. In the dining room, fresh vegetables are the rule, and a special "taste-of-England" menu is presented.

Flowers bloom in the gardens of Peacock Vane, as on all the Isle of Wight, about three weeks before they do on the mainland. There is a very old Norman church in the village, and it is said of its churchyard, where Swinburne was buried in 1909, "It might make one in love with death to think one would be buried in so sweet a place."

Proprietors: The Wolfenden family. *Closed:* Mid-November through February, except weekends. *Recreational facilities:* Outdoor pool at the hotel; ocean swimming, riding, and tennis a short drive away. *Other facilities:* Lounge, cocktail bar, garden. *Rooms:* 6 with bath and TV. 3-day midweek reduction. No children under 7. Moderate. *Restaurant service:* Luncheon (except Monday and Tuesday), dinner. *Credit cards:* Amex, Diners, Master, Visa. *How to get there:* Ferries run to the Isle of Wight from Lymington, Portsmouth, and Southampton, which can all be reached by train from Waterloo Station, London. A reservation well ahead for an auto is essential weekends and all summer. There are local buses for transportation on the island, and cars can be rented there. *Telephone:* (0983) 852019.

WINTERBOURNE HOTEL

My dear Kate,
I have taken a most delightful house . . . at Bonchurch
—cool, airy, private bathing, everything delicious—I
think it is the prettiest place I ever saw in my life. . . .
The man with the post bag is swearing in the passage.
Ever affectionately,
C.D.
A water fall on the grounds which I have arranged
with a carpenter to convert into a perpetual shower bath.
Charles Dickens, 1849

A photostat of the original of the letter quoted above is framed at the Winterbourne. The waterfall is still in the garden, and a zigzag path descends the cliffs to the beach, where we bought sandwiches made from freshly steamed crab. There are glorious ocean views from the garden terrace and from some bedrooms, all named for Dicken's characters—Peggotty, Trot, Micawber, and so forth. Here the famous author wrote *David Copperfield.* Very much a family man, he had been searching for a rental in a healthy climate for his "chickens."

This lovely house is very well furnished and quite luxurious, with fine modern bathrooms. Guests mix easily here. The Isle of Wight is beautiful and worth the trip. Bonchurch has more than once won an award as the "Best Kept Village."

Proprietors: Douglas and Betty Goodchild. *Closed:* January and February. *Recreational facilities:* Outdoor pool and ocean swimming at the hotel; golf, tennis, squash, fishing, boat rental, boat trips, deep-sea fishing, and riding a short drive away. *Other facilities:* Drawing room, TV lounge, cocktail bar, garden. *Rooms:* 19 with bath and TV. 2-day breaks. Christmas program. No children under 7; reduction for children sharing. Moderate to expensive. *Restaurant service:* Snacks, tea, and dinner. *Credit cards:* Amex, Diners, Master, Visa. *How to get there:* Ferries run to the Isle of Wight from Lymington, Portsmouth, and Southampton, which can all be reached by train from Waterloo Station, London. A reservation well ahead for an auto is essential weekends and all summer. There are local buses for transportation on the island, and cars can be rented there. *Telephone:* (0983) 852535.

MILLSTREAM HOTEL

> Bosham, my good Herbert,
> Thy birthplace — the sea-creek — the petty rill
> That falls into it — the green field — the grey church.
> *Alfred, Lord Tennyson,* 1849

Although the Millstream's roots date from 1701, when it was a malt house, it is tastefully decorated in light and airy contemporary colors, and such amenities as modern carpeted bathrooms are strictly twentieth century.

Bosham, favored by yachtsmen and the loveliest village we saw on the south coast of England, offers more than beauty. It was probably the English headquarters of King Canute, the Dane who conquered England in 1016. His little daughter is thought to be buried in the venerable church that still survives, one of the very few Saxon churches remaining in Britain. Harold, the last Saxon king of England — killed by William's army at that famous battle in 1066 — had a manor here. From the Millstream in Bosham center, walk to the waterfront street, where any auto left parked too long is completely covered when the unusually high tide floods in daily. The cluster of boats in the placid blue harbor may invite you to hire one and try some sailing yourself.

The dining room at the Millstream serves excellent meals, and the attractive bar, furnished with cane, draws visiting yachtsmen. One American told us this was his favorite lodging on a tour throughout England.

Manager: Nicholas and Lesley Barker. *Recreational facilities:* Sailing instruction, boat rental, boat trips, and deep-sea fishing a short walk away; riding a short drive away. *Other facilities:* Lounge, cocktail bar, garden. *Rooms:* 22 with bath, telephone, tea-making, and TV. 2-day reduction. Moderate. *Restaurant service:* Luncheon, tea, dinner. *Credit cards:* Amex, Diners, Master, Visa. *How to get there:* Turn south off Route A27, 4 miles west of Chichester. Guests can be met at the Bosham railway station. *Telephone:* (0243) 573 234. *Agent in the United States:* Best Western. [T]

WILLMEAD FARM

> A Devonshire cottage...crushed beneath its burden of
> thatch...it seems to be stationed there for no more ob-
> vious purpose than to keep a promise to your fancy.
> *Henry James,* 1872

A visit to Willmead Farm captures, if briefly, a moment in the rural past. At this charmer you'll find great atmosphere, log fires, and a warm welcome from Hilary Roberts, a widow.

The house dates back to the fourteenth century. One room is a medieval hall with minstrels' gallery. In it is a grandfather clock that towers high into the two-story room. The living room has big comfortable chairs and sofa in front of a massive stone fireplace, decked with gleaming copper and brass. Paintings and blue and white china decorate traditional white plaster walls. Magazines are on antique tables, and shelves hold books. Bring any spirits you might want to sip during an evening.

The dining room is a step down from the living room, open to it and set off by enormous rough beams. Large Chippendale chairs surround a table where guests have breakfast together. For dinner—none served at the house—you can walk along a footpath to a village restaurant or drive a few miles to nearby country-house hotels. A cozy old world awaits you at Willmead Farm.

Proprietor: Hilary Roberts. *Closed:* Christmas and New Year weeks. *Facilities:* Living room, lounge, garden. *Rooms:* 3 sharing baths. No children under 10. Very inexpensive. *How to get there:* From Bovey Tracey, take Route A382 toward Moretonhampstead. Take the first left past the Hawkmoor Hospital and continue 1/2 mile. *Telephone:* (06477) 214.

Brampton, Cumbria

FARLAM HALL

> Thirty feet high is the Wall . . . but the Wall itself is not
> more wonderful than the town behind it . . . a thin town
> eighty miles long. Think of it! One roaring rioting town.
> . . . On one side heather, woods and ruins where Picts
> hide, and on the other, a vast town—long like a snake,
> and wicked like a snake. *Rudyard Kipling, 1906*

Close enough to Hadrian's Wall to have been part of the wicked city
described by Kipling above, Farlam Hall is a place to spend a few days

while you explore this lovely rolling farm country that has such a fascinating past. A warm reception greets guests at this country-house hotel for people who like quiet.

The building is listed as of historical and architectural interest (John Wesley is reputed to have preached in the house), and is furnished in keeping. In the lounge there is a tile-faced fireplace, as well as upholstered pieces in cretonne and velvet beside antique tables that hold unusual English magazines. Up a winding stairway are warmly carpeted, well-furnished bedrooms; attention to detail is meticulous. In exceptionally pretty gardens, ducklings swim on a little pond and bluebells grow along a stream with a tiny stone bridge.

Son Barry Quinion offers Cordon Bleu cooking, using only the best of materials prepared with great care. The set menu provides a choice of three entrées, one of which is usually something unusual, such as wood pigeon braised in red wine or saddle of roast hare. Lobster soup or prawn and avocado salad might start the meal. Many residents of the area come in for dinner, chatting with Alan Quinion as he dispenses drinks in the attractive small bar. In an atmosphere well-mannered but not formal, coat and tie are preferred but not requisite.

Proprietors: The Quinion family. *Closed:* February and Christmas. *Recreational facilities:* Lake swimming and riding a short drive away. *Other facilities:* Lounge, cocktail bar, garden. *Rooms:* 13 with bath and TV. Ground floor rooms. Winter breaks. Moderate to expensive. *Restaurant service:* Dinner. *Credit cards:* Amex, Master, Visa. *How to get there:* Farlam Hall is on Route A689, 2½ miles east of Brampton, on the road to Alston. *Telephone:* (069 76) 234.

Branscombe, Devon

YE OLDE MASONS ARMS

It beckoned "Come In!" with every breath of air.
Charles Dickens

The lingering associations of an old smugglers' haunt cling to this four-teenth-century inn, for this was the hangout of the Branscombe smugglers, always referred to as the "gentlemen," as in Rudyard Kipling's poem "A Smuggler's Song." Children were taught to ignore sounds of voices in the night or muffled steps of a horse that should have been quiet in its stable.

The word "quaint" could have been coined for the Masons Arms. You may stop for a snack lunch on the lawn, where you will sit under a thatched umbrella that matches the thatched roofs of many of the houses in this captivating village, the property of King Alfred in the ninth century. The South Sea Islands look is quite unexpected in England. Some bedrooms are in converted cottages across the road from the ancient inn.

This lodging will best suit those who enjoy socializing in a friendly bar. The attractive upstairs lounge seems almost unused, as we have found is frequently true of lounges above the main floor. No other hotel guest came in while we spent an evening reading there.

Branscombe continues a lace-making industry just as in the days when it had the honor of supplying Queen Alexandra's wedding dress. While here you will be in the stream of English life from long ago to the present, but with all of today's comforts.

Proprietor: Janet Inglis. *Recreational facilities:* Ocean swimming a short walk away; riding a short drive away. *Facilities for children:* Baby-listening. *Other facilities:* Lounge, public bar, garden. *Rooms:* 21, 14 with bath. Winter breaks; Christmas program. Minimum 2-night advance reservation in season. Ground-floor rooms. Inexpensive to moderate. *Restaurant service:* Snacks, tea, dinner. *How to get there:* Take Route A3052 from Lyme Regis west to B3774 to Seaton. From there travel west along the coast to Branscombe. *Telephone:* (029 780) 300.

Broadway, Hereford and Worcester

BROADWAY HOTEL

> Broadway is the very pattern of the old English village
> one sees on the stage.
>
> *Richard Le Gallienne,* 1900

The Broadway will call "Come in" to you. The architecture of the half-timbered, fifteenth-century building, with its two-story beamed and balconied lounge, offers so much atmosphere that you'll forgive the modern furnishings that predominate in the bedrooms. Formerly owned by the Abbots of Pershore, it has a garden where teas are served and a cheerful bar with traditional red carpet, diamond-paned windows, timbered ceiling, and horse brasses decorating the massive chimney beam.

Those who want to take a train out of London for an English country experience will enjoy walks through the streets of this village of golden Cotswold stone. Fine shops for browsing display antiques, quality gifts, clothes, books, and foodstuffs. Day trips to neighboring towns and villages can be made by local bus.

In season Broadway is jammed and the hotel will not accept advance booking for just one night.

Manager: Mrs. P. Swinden. *Recreational facilities:* Riding a short drive away. *Other facilities:* Lounge, public bar, garden. *Rooms:* 24, 22 with bath, all with telephone, TV, and tea-making. Winter breaks. Moderate. *Restaurant service:* Luncheon, snacks, tea, dinner. *Credit cards:* Amex, Diners, Master, Visa. *How to get there:* Broadway is southwest of Stratford on Route A46. Guests will be met at the Evesham railway station without charge. *Telephone:* (0386) 852401.   [T]

COLLIN HOUSE HOTEL

Take from this hearth its warmth,
From this room its charm,
From this inn its amity,
Return them not, but return.

Anonymous

Warmth, charm, and amity are keynotes at Collin House. The friendly sixteenth-century stone house has been carefully restored to retain its character. We had lunch in a beamed bar, sitting on armchairs grouped around an inglenook fireplace where a log fire burned even in the morning. In a candlelit dining room, walls are hung with original paintings, and mullion windows look out on a garden. The menu is varied, and the food is outstanding.

Well-carpeted bedrooms come with comfortable chairs, shoe-cleaning and sewing kits, and biscuits to nibble on; each has a book made up of information about the area, with brochures and suggestions of things to do. Two have four-poster beds, and those on the third floor are very romantic, heavily raftered, and open to peaked ceilings.

John spends a great deal of time helping guests map out their plans for the day, routing them along the most pleasing country lanes to whatever their interests. If these include antiques and paintings, he will direct guests to the best antique shops and galleries.

The setting is peaceful, in eight acres of garden about a mile away from the crowds that are drawn to the picture-postcard Cotswold village of Broadway. This is a place to spend more than overnight. Just thinking about it has us wishing we could be there tomorrow.

Proprietors: John and Judith Mills. *Closed:* 3 days at Christmas. *Recreational facilities:* Outdoor pool at the hotel; riding, hunting, and golf nearby. *Other facilities:* Lounge, cocktail lounge, garden. *Rooms:* 7 with bath. Moderate. *Restaurant service:* Luncheon, snacks, and dinner. *Credit cards:* Master, Visa. *How to get there:* Take Route A44 northwest from Broadway. Turn right onto Collin Lane. The hotel is on the right. *Telephone:* (0386) 858354.

LYGON ARMS

> We put up at a most comfortable cleanly house where a delicious loyn of veal was ready, and I was ready for eating it; which I did in ample quantity, and had then a superabundant temptation by an apricot tart.
>
> *John Byng,* 1787

Thus did the author describe the Lygon Arms. Its exact age is unknown, but much of it was built by men who were alive two hundred years before the Mayflower sailed for America. The year of that voyage, 1620, is carved over the main entrance, added when the old coaching inn was enlarged. It is carved also in the headboard of a four-poster in one of the old chambers used today.

There are two modern wings in the extensive rear garden, beautifully designed with every modern convenience, but if you want to slip into

another century you will ask to lodge in the inn's medieval section, where some bedrooms have walls 4 feet thick, some have fireplaces, and all are furnished with antiques. A silk-hosed gallant in powdered wig would feel right at home — that is, until he opened the door to the luxurious adjoining bathroom.

Legend has it that Oliver Cromwell slept here just before the Battle of Worcester in 1651. The inn has played host to Charles I and, much more recently, to the present duke of Edinburgh. The antiques in the public rooms are treasures, especially two tables, one from the seventeenth century and one Elizabethan, both featured in *The Dictionary of English Furniture*.

There is a four-day Christmas celebration when carols are sung by candlelight in the galleried Great Hall and guests join for hot toddy and mince pies after midnight mass in the village. In addition to the traditional Christmas dinner, there are two black-tie dinners, Christmas games, and teas.

Broadway is home to the Cotswold Hunt, and the Hunt Ball is held each December at the inn. The Lygon Arms, possibly the most famous country inn in Britain, lives on graciously from one long continuous past into the bustling present, a hotel full of smartly dressed people who demand the most modern luxuries while enjoying English history.

Proprietor: D.J. Barrington. *Recreational facilities:* Tennis at the hotel; riding, hunting, squash, and indoor pool a short drive away. *Other facilities:* Lounges, TV lounge, cocktail bar, public bar, garden, gift shop. *Rooms:* 67 with bath, TV, and telephone. Suitable for wheelchair guests. 2-day reduction; Christmas program. Very expensive. *Restaurant service:* Luncheon, early and late snacks, tea, dinner. *Credit cards:* Amex, Carte Blanche, Diners, Master, Visa. *How to get there:* Broadway is southwest of Stratford on Route A46. Take a bus from Waterloo Station, London, to Broadway. Car rental available locally. *Telephone:* (0386) 852 255. *Agents in the United States:* David Mitchell, Scott Calder. [T]

BAY TREE

O Fair is Moreton in the Marsh
And Stow on the wide wold
But fairer far is Burford town
With its stone roofs grey and old

H.C. Beeching

This was the home of Sir Laurence Tanfield, the unpopular lord chief baron of the Exchequer for Elizabeth I, so it's likely that she visited the Bay Tree when she was in Burford in 1574. The past lives everywhere around you at this inn. Oak paneling, enormous log-burning fireplaces, and a minstrel's gallery are but a few of the architectural delights. The house is built around a miniature courtyard, and behind it lies a garden with sun loggia, stone terraces, and a lily pond. A little bar is tucked under the stairs, and there is a library for quiet browsing.

As you stroll along the wide High Street, which leads down to the River Windrush, you'll see handsome houses built when the town flourished with the wool trade. The architecture is different from that of most Cotswold towns—half-timbering on brown stone—as there was wood available from the Forest of Wychwood. You may begin to imagine yourself on a stage set and think you hear coaches and horses clattering along the cobblestones.

Proprietors: Mr. and Mrs. Peter King. *Recreational facilities:* Golf a short walk away. *Other facilities:* 3 lounges, library, cocktail bar, garden. *Rooms:* 23 with bath and TV. 3-day reduction; winter weekends November through March; reduction for children under 12 sharing. Inexpensive to moderate. *Restaurant service:* Luncheon, tea, dinner. *How to get there:* Burford is on Route A361 between Chipping Norton and Swindon. Trains can be met at the Charlbury station. Bus from Victoria Station, London, almost to the hotel door; get off on High Street, at corner of Sheep Street. Car rental available locally. *Telephone:* (099 382) 3137.

RED LION HOTEL

> Happier life I cannot imagine than this vagrancy...and towards evening a courteous welcome in a rustic inn.
> *Thomas De Quincy,* 1807

In a picturesque moorland village with a maypole on its village green, the Red Lion stands on the bank of the River Wharfe. A village churchyard has Viking gravestones, and the famous Bolton Abbey is nearby. This plain, well-run little inn, with a friendly staff and a garden, might be a convenient stopover for those driving gypsy style, without advance reservations.

Although Burnsall is a peaceful place during the week, we'd avoid it on a weekend, when it's mobbed with holiday-makers from the cities to the south and families crowd the Red Lion at noon to enjoy its traditional Sunday roast-beef dinner.

Proprietor: Mr. Leslie Warnett. *Special facilities:* Lounge, TV lounge, public bar, garden. *Rooms:* 12, 2 with bath. 2-day reduction; 2-day winter breaks; reduction for children under 13 sharing. Inexpensive. *Restaurant service:* Snacks and dinner. *How to get there:* Burnsall is on Route B6160, north of Bolton Abbey. *Telephone:* (075 672) 204.

ANGEL HOTEL

> "And this," said Mr. Pickwick, looking up, "is the Angel! We alight here, Sam."
>
> *Charles Dickens,* 1837

Dickens had quite an affection for "the bright little town of Bury St Edmunds." He visited the Angel Hotel twice to give readings, and you can stay today in the "fine room" where he slept, preserved, with a four-poster bed, as it was more than a century ago. In *The Pickwick Papers* he immortalized the Angel as the place where Sam Weller first ran into Job Trotter.

The hotel's two dining rooms, one in a medieval vaulted cellar, are recommended in English food guides. Roast beef from a huge joint, rolled to your table and kept warm under a big silver dome, is carved to your order. The wine list is above average.

Town records first mention the Angel as an inn in 1452. Most of the present ivy-covered building dates from 1779. This busy hotel looks across the road at the massive gate to public gardens that surround romantic ruins of an eleventh-century abbey founded by King Canute. The historic market town is a fine place for a train traveler, as there is so much to see here.

Manager: Andrew Donovan. *Recreational facilities:* Tennis, indoor pool, squash, sauna, and riding nearby. *Facilities for children:* Baby-listening. *Other facilities:* 2 lounges, cocktail bar, public bar. *Rooms:* 41 with bath, telephone, and TV. Weekend breaks November 1–May 1; discount for children sharing. Moderate to expensive. *Restaurant service:* Luncheon, snacks, tea, dinner. *Credit cards:* Amex, Diners, Master, Visa. *How to get there:* The town can be reached by train and bus (coach). *Telephone:* (0284) 3926. *Agent in the United States:* Josephine Barr. [T]

Canterbury, Kent

FALSTAFF HOTEL

from every shires ende
of Engelond, to Caunterbury they wende,
The holy blisful martir for to seke.

Geoffrey Chaucer, 1388

The Falstaff Hotel had not yet been built when Chaucer told tales of the pilgrims he brought together to wend their way from London to Canterbury. At that time the gates of the town were locked as darkness fell. Those who arrived late, perhaps from much feasting and story-telling along the way, had to lie under the walls of the medieval town until morning. In 1403, the Falstaff went up just outside the Westgate to house such laggards. Today it is part of central Canterbury and a short walk from the cathedral.

The character that for centuries has attracted the traveler is emphasized by the inn's black and white timbered upper stories that overhang the street, its mullioned windows, and its early paneling and heavy beams secured by wooden pegs. One room has a four-poster, but others have unit furniture and good modern bathrooms. Public rooms are properly atmospheric but rather impersonal, to be expected in a town as bustling as Canterbury. The dining room is busy, serving locals and tourists alike. It was intriguing to learn that the word "canter" derives from a description of the easy lope of the horses the pilgrims rode across the downs on their way to Canterbury.

Manager: Rolf Steinmetz. *Special facilities:* Lounge, public bar, parking. *Rooms:* 24 with bath, TV, telephone, and tea-making. Weekend breaks all year. Moderate. *Restaurant service:* Luncheon, snacks, dinner. *Credit cards:* Amex, Diners, Visa. *How to get there:* The hotel is on St. Dunstan's Street. Take train from Charing Cross station, London, to Canterbury West Station, which is 400 yards from the hotel. *Telephone:* (0227) 462138.

AYNSOME MANOR

> Hospitality without formality
> With heartiness and cordiality.
>
> *Anonymous*

Decorated with antiques and charm, the old manor is far more beautiful inside than its rather severe exterior might lead you to expect. The remarkable freestanding spiral staircase of stone, genuine Adam, is a beauty, as are the Adam fireplace and elaborately molded Adam ceiling.

This is an ideal spot for the single traveler, especially one who does not care to drive alone. The owners, the Varleys, will not only meet guests at the train but will cart them around while they go about their daily errands. Anyone is welcome to jump into the car wherever they go. Tony Varley and his head chef were recently filmed at Aynsome Manor by the BBC for an international-cooking series. A single room is just half the price of a double.

Proprietors: The Varley family. *Closed:* January 2–22. *Recreational facilities:* Outdoor saltwater pool, ocean and lake swimming, tennis, riding, golf, and trout fishing a short drive away. *Other facilities:* 2 lounges, TV lounge, cocktail bar, garden. *Rooms:* 16, 13 with bath. 3-day reduction; reduction for children sharing; winter breaks; Christmas program. 1 twin-bedded ground-floor room. Inexpensive to moderate. *Restaurant service:* Dinner. *Credit cards:* Amex, Master, Visa. *How to get there:* Take Route A590 to signs for Cartmel. The hotel is north of the village center. Guests can be met at the Grange-over-Sands railway station. *Telephone:* (044 854) 276.   [T]

Chagford, Devon

GIDLEIGH PARK

There are wastes and wilds, crags of granite, views into far-off districts, and the sound of waters hurrying away over their rocky beds, enough to satisfy the largest hungering and thirsting after poetical delight. I shall never forget the feelings of delicious entrancement with which I approached the outskirts of Dartmoor.

William Howitt, 1841

Gidleigh Park is one of the most peaceful and secluded hotels in Britain.

Set 700 feet high on the edge of Dartmoor, in wastes and wilds and crags of granite, protected on three sides and offering magnificent views on the fourth, it is a mile and a half up a very narrow lane from the nearest road. Terraced gardens step down to the Teign River, which you can hear in the night as it hurries away over its rocky bed.

Paul and Kay Henderson are Americans, Kay from Indiana, Paul brought up in a military family that moved around the country. They met while at Purdue University. When a job took them to London in 1970, they spent vacations visiting Michelin 3-star restaurants and staying in the best small English country hotels. Kay went to Cordon Bleu classes in London and Paris and taught a cooking class in her London home.

When they bought Gidleigh Park in 1977, their aim was to develop a perfect country inn with "English country-house atmosphere, French food, and American plumbing." That they soon succeeded is attested by the awards and accolades showered on them by food guides, wine associations, and European publications. The *American Wine Spectator* gave Gidleigh Park a "Grand Award" for having the best wine list in Britain. More significant, perhaps, is that over half the guests are returnees.

The mansion was built by a shipping magnate in 1928 as a country retreat. Oak-paneled public rooms are furnished with antiques, comfortable seating, deep-piled carpets, and fresh flowers. Fires burn winter and summer. Bedrooms, some with balconies, rate high on comfort. The Hendersons are welcoming and mix with their guests. Relaxed informality is the rule.

Besides the wonderful food and wine, you'll find "character, courtesy, calm, comfort," the attributes that made Gidleigh Park qualify to join the prestigious Relais et Chateaux association.

Proprietors: Kay and Paul Henderson. *Recreational facilities:* Tennis at the hotel; outdoor pool, river swimming (for the daring), riding, golf, and windsurfing nearby. *Facilities for children:* Baby-sitting. *Other facilities:* Hall lounge, drawing room, cocktail bar, garden. *Rooms:* 12 with bath, telephone, and TV. No children under 12 except infants. Expensive to very expensive. *Restaurant service:* Luncheon, snacks, tea, and dinner. *Credit card:* Amex. *How to get there:* From Chagford Square, face Webbers, with Lloyds Bank on your right. Turn right into Mill Street. After 200 yards, turn to the right and go downhill to Factory Crossroad. Go straight across into Holy Street and follow the lane 1 1/2 miles to the end. Do not go into Gidleigh. *Telephone:* (06473) 2367. *Agent in the United States:* David Mitchell.   [T]

MILL END HOTEL

> Wild Dartmoor! thou that midst thy mountains rude
> Hast robed thyself with haughty solitude.
>
> *Felicia Hemans*

The Mill End Hotel is a converted old mill, a fine example of adaptive preservation. Afternoon tea in the lounge, a cheerful blaze of wood fire on the hearth, is a charming English experience. Soft chairs and couches are slipcovered in flowered English linen; tables hold fresh flowers and copies of *Country Life;* a chess board is set up ready for play. When it's time for a drink before dinner, there is a brass gong to strike for service. After the first "bong," guests come drifting in, and everyone talks to everyone else.

Unusual dishes on the menu merit comment. Hors d'oeuvres might be finnan haddock in cheese sauce or fresh tomato mousse before a main course of roast pheasant, guinea fowl, or squab and mushroom pie. Then the sweets trolley rolls up laden with Sacher torte, gooseberry gateau,

Duke of Cambridge tart — "and wouldn't you like to try some of each, Madam?" For unadventurous souls, more usual dishes are beautifully presented.

The third-floor bedrooms have beams, the more modern ones on the ground floor have individual terraces. Colorful chairs on the lawn invite lounging where rooks circle over the sun-dappled river. All of this loveliness is in Dartmoor National Park. You can travel far over its rugged, lonely moors and meet only sheep and wild ponies.

Proprietor: Nicholas Craddock. *Closed:* Late December. *Recreational facilities:* River swimming at the hotel; outdoor pool a short walk away; hunting and indoor and outdoor riding a short drive away. *Facilities for children:* Children's supper. *Other facilities:* Drawing room, lounge, cocktail bar, garden. *Rooms:* 16 with bath, TV, and telephone. Ground-floor rooms. Off-season rates; 2-day reduction; children under 16 free if sharing, 10% discount if in separate room. Moderate. *Restaurant service:* Luncheon, tea, dinner. *Credit cards:* Amex, Diners, Master, Visa. *How to get there:* Take Route A30 from Exeter to A382. Find Mill End signposted on A382. Do not turn into the village of Chagford. *Telephone:* (06473) 2282.

Cheltenham, Gloucestershire

HOTEL DE LA BERE

... the large and spacious houses, with their oriel, latticed windows, their huge fireplaces and their gabled roofs, breathe of the days of hose and doublet, of pearl-embroidered stomachers, and complicated oaths.

Jerome K. Jerome, 1889

This manor was already old when Shakespeare was born not far away. Its great hall and minstrel gallery probably echoed to the performance of his plays, acted by the strolling players who performed at inns and manor houses as was the custom of the time. Today it is a rare combination of ancient house and fine sporting facilities that will be enjoyed by those who like to keep active as they tour. Within its stone walls and on its sweeping lawns, with their magnificent old trees and formal gardens, are four tennis courts, five squash courts, a large outdoor swimming pool, and a pitch-and-putt golf course.

The house was built at the time of the Wars of the Roses. Its spacious bedrooms, some crossbeamed with high slanting ceilings, others with four-poster beds (and also some with modern furniture), are named for English kings and queens, some of whom probably slept in them. Rare oak paneling, ornate plasterwork, open fires in huge hearths, and massive timberwork evoke the pageantry of Tudor days. Cuisine is first-class, and bread and pastries are baked in the kitchen. An exceptional wine selection is in all price ranges, as the hotel's owner is a confrere of the Chevaliers du Tastevin.

Southam is a small village 2 miles from the Regency town of Cheltenham Spa, with fine shopping, outdoor cafés, and antique stores set along wide promenades. The hotel overlooks the Cheltenham racecourse. For those who like to get in a daily game or swim, this unique hotel is a center for such attractions as Bath, Stratford, Oxford, and the romantic Cotswold villages.

Manager: S. John Harrison. *Closed:* A few days for New Year's. *Recreational facilities:* Tennis, squash, outdoor pool, pitch-and-putt golf course, indoor tennis and badminton, sauna, gymnasium, dancing Friday and Saturday nights at the hotel; riding nearby. *Facilities for children:* baby-listening; children's meals. *Other facilities:* Several lounges, cocktail bar, public bar, garden. *Rooms:* 34 with bath, TV, telephone, and tea-making. 2-day reduction; discount for children sharing (under 3 free). Christmas program. Moderate. *Restaurant service:* Luncheon, snacks, tea, dinner. *Credit cards:* Amex, Diners, Master, Visa. *How to get there:* The hotel is on A46, 2 miles northeast of Cheltenham in Southam village. *Telephone:* (0242) 37771. *Agents in the United States:* Best Western and Ray Morrow. [T]

Chipping Campden, Gloucestershire

KINGS ARMS

And there is Chipping Campden . . . which fortunately
is still a real little town and not simply a show place and
glorified tea establishment for tourists. There is no Ye
Olde Chipping Campden nonsense about it.

J. B. Priestley, 1934

This Georgian hotel, personally run by the owner, stands in the square by
the medieval covered outdoor market hall on what historian Sir George
Trevelyan called the "most beautiful village street in England." The
house is handsome, with friendly service. Oriental rugs on polished
floors lead to an attractive old bar and beyond it to a garden. Fresh
flowers and fruit in the bedrooms, furnished to reflect the period but not
centrally heated, add to the feeling of gracious hospitality.

The dining room receives rosettes in English food guides and offers
an unusual service — late suppers for those who want to attend the
Shakespeare plays in Stratford, only 12 miles away. Chipping Campden
is one of the most beautiful of the Cotswold villages, and the Kings Arms
is so agreeable that you may want to make it your center for a long visit.

Proprietor: Alexander Guthrie. *Recreational facilities:* Riding, golf,
and tennis nearby. *Other facilities:* Lounge, cocktail bar, garden.
Rooms: 14, 2 with bath. 3-day reduction; winter breaks; Christmas pro-
gram. Inexpensive to moderate. *Restaurant service:* Snacks, dinner.
Credit cards: Master, Visa. *How to get there:* Chipping Campden is on
Route B4081, which runs off A44 between Broadway and Moreton-in-
Marsh. *Telephone:* (0386) 840 256.   [T]

Climping, West Sussex

BAILIFFSCOURT HOTEL

I know not how it is with you—
I love the first and last,
The whole field of the present view,
The whole flow of the past.

Robert Louis Stevenson, 1883

This medieval-looking house was built just over a half century ago, at tremendous cost, to satisfy a whim of Lord Moyne's. On a thousand-acre estate bordering the sea, he found a moat surrounding the site of a courthouse tended by bailiff monks in the twelfth century. To restore this bailiffs' court, Britain was scoured for features from ancient buildings: a molded oaken ceiling from a rectory, ceiling beams from a barn, an ancient door with its original lock and hinge from a stable, medieval windows rescued from deserted abbeys and manors. Stones and timbers from the original courthouse were found embedded in derelict farm buildings on the estate. Arches, doorways, quoins, and windows were carefully restored for the new building, four-sided around a square courtyard. Architecturally correct, Bailiffscourt is one of the most beautiful and expensive fakes in the world.

Since 1948 it has been a romantic luxury hotel. Eight bedrooms have four-posters with floral hangings; nine have working fireplaces. Medieval wooden furniture is combined with comfortable tapestry and velvet-covered chairs and sofas. Bathrooms, however, are luxuriously twentieth century.

In summer a cold buffet luncheon may be enjoyed in a rose-clad courtyard or a walled garden. Christmas at Bailiffscourt evokes "merrie olde England," with mulled wine before log fires in great stone fireplaces and parties under rough-hewn oaken beams. New Year's brings another festive program. With tennis courts, sauna, exercise room, and both a beach and a pool, this is a place to stay and relax for a few days in the midst of a busy tour.

Proprietors: Fiona and Tim Lamming. *Recreational facilities:* Ocean swimming, outdoor pool, tennis, sauna, and exercise room at the hotel; riding, sailing, and windsurfing nearby. *Other facilities:* Lounge, cocktail bar, garden, helicopter landing pad. *Rooms:* 18 with bath, TV, and telephone; 2 cottages. Midweek reduction. No children under 10. Expensive to very expensive. *Restaurant service:* Luncheon, tea, dinner. *Credit cards:* Amex, Diners, Master, Visa. *How to get there:* Take Route A284 from just south of Arundel. Turn right onto Route A259. The hotel is on the first road to the left, near Littlehampton. *Telephone:* (0903) 723511. [T]

Constantine Bay, Cornwall

TREGLOS HOTEL

> The restless Atlantic is ever thundering on this iron-walled coast.
>
> *Sabine Baring-Gould,* 1876

From our bedroom window we watched the Atlantic thunder on this coast. We enjoyed feeling snug while the wind howled outside, drifting to sleep with the sound of the waves and the smell of the sea.

This well-kept seaside hotel, not at all quaint but very pleasant, is set well back from the ocean on an unspoiled part of the busy Cornwall coast, away from the summer crowds at the seaside resort towns. The building is late nineteenth-century with later additions. Furnishings in the sunny public rooms seem to have evolved over the years without any help from decorators. The effect is cheerful and friendly, especially when fires are lit. Plain bedrooms in light colors have unit furniture—ask for one facing the sea. Bed boards are available, and your shoes will be polished if you leave them outside your door. The staff is friendly and solicitous, influenced, no doubt, by the caring attitude of the owners, Ted and Barbara Barlow.

If you are traveling with teen-agers, they'd welcome a few days here to enjoy all the sporting facilities. Younger children are well provided for, too. The hotel's guests are automatically social members of the Trevose Golf Course (adjoining the hotel), which includes free use of the outdoor pool and reduced rates in early and late season for golf and tennis.

Proprietors: Barbara and Ted Barlow. *Closed:* November to mid-March. *Recreational facilities:* Outdoor pool, indoor pool, ocean swimming, surfing, boat trips, golf, tennis, and Jacuzzi at the hotel or club; riding, boat rental, water-skiing, and fishing for mackerel, bass, pollack, and shark nearby. *Facilities for children:* Baby-sitting and -listening, games room, and children's meals. *Other facilities:* 2 lounges, card room, snooker room, cocktail bar, laundry facilities, sun terrace, garden. *Rooms:* 44 with bath, telephone, and TV; 4 self-catering flats. Suitable for wheel-chair guests. Off-season rates. Expensive. *Restaurant service:* Luncheon, snacks, tea, dinner (coat and tie). *How to get there:* Constantine Bay is signposted on the coast road, Route B3276, between Padstow and Newquay. *Telephone:* (0841) 520727.

Cornhill-on-Tweed, Northumberland

TILLMOUTH PARK

From Flodden ridge
The Scots beheld the English host
Leave Barmoor Wood, their evening post
And heedful watched them as they crossed
The Till by Twizel Bridge.

Sir Walter Scott

The map of the border region between England and Scotland contains
many crossed swords denoting ancient battlefields and shows the strong-
holds from which the border lords once made their sorties. It was across
Twizel Bridge, on the Tillmouth Park estate, that Lord Surrey led the
English artillery on the fateful morning of the Battle of Flodden in 1513.

At the mouth of the Till on the English bank of the River Tweed,
which defines the border with Scotland, is this magnificent Victorian

mansion surrounded by a 1,000-acre estate. The entrance hall is impressive — oak balcony, stained glass, framed tapestries, and a 43-pound mounted salmon caught by Lady Burnet, the nonresident owner of Tillmouth Park. The galleried drawing room, with a massive stone fireplace and deep armchairs, would make a fine setting for an Agatha Christie mystery. It's easy to picture Hercule Poirot gathering all the guests at a house party together for questioning here. The Sir Walter Scott bedroom is magnificent, and all are spacious, with memories of more formal days. One has a four-poster. With the good central heating, the electric fires in fireplaces and electric blankets are not necessary, but they are cozy.

Velvety lawns with croquet and putting green surround the hotel. Salmon leap in the rivers Till and Tweed, which flow through the estate, with fishing rights controlled by the hotel. Guests should book in advance to reserve a boat on either river to go after salmon or sea trout, but the manager can usually arrange for brown trout or coarse fishing at short notice.

Northumberland is a beautiful county of prosperous farmland, less well known to Americans than many parts of England. It is a pleasure to drive through it and end the day at distinguished Tillmouth Park.

Managers: Tony and Christine Brooks-Sykes. *Recreational facilities:* Fishing and river swimming at the hotel; tennis, riding, and hunting a short drive away. *Facilities for children:* Baby-sitting and-listening. *Other facilities:* Drawing room, TV lounge, cocktail bar, public bar, game room. *Rooms:* 14, 7 with bath and TV. New Year's program; reduction for children. Moderate. *Restaurant service:* Luncheon, early and late snacks, dinner. *Credit cards:* Amex, Diners, Master, Visa. *How to get there:* Cornhill-on-Tweed is on Route A697 between Coldstream and Crookham. From the village center take A698 to Tillmouth Park. *Telephone:* (0890) 2255.   [T]

Coxwold, Yorkshire

FAUCONBERG ARMS

> Coxwold . . . is really a show village, a picture of mellowness and grace with a fine inn, the Fauconberg Arms.
> *James Herriot*, 1979

A more attractive little inn would be hard to find: traditional white walls, red rugs, heavy black beams, a wealth of old blue and white china, a Welsh dresser loaded with antiques. Add to this a setting in an enchanting village, a warm welcome, a friendly atmosphere, and first-class cuisine. Who could ask for more?

Bedrooms are prettily done up with matching wallpapers, spreads, and sheets by Sanderson. Even the ceilings are papered, and all is spotlessly maintained. The largest bedroom has a shower built into one corner.

Silvery stone houses line the broad street of Coxwold, a Domesday Book village where Laurence Sterne was rector. Here he wrote most of *Tristram Shandy* in a house now open as a Sterne museum. Nearby is Ampleforth Abbey, a famous Benedictine school, where we attended mass and heard the schoolboy choir. The Cistercian ruins of Byland and Rievaulx abbeys and Newburgh Priory, where Oliver Cromwell's remains are hidden, are all within a few miles.

This snug retreat should be on every inn lover's list.

Proprietors: Dick and Tricia Goodall. *Special facilities:* Bar lounge. *Rooms:* 4 sharing baths. Inexpensive. *Restaurant service:* Luncheon, snacks, dinner. Closed Mondays. *How to get there:* Coxwold is east of Route A19 at the very southern tip of the North Yorkshire moors, southwest of Helmsley. *Telephone:* (034 76) 214.

MANOR FARM

So bright and lovely is the dear old place,
It seems as though the country's very heart
Were centered here, and that its antique grace
Must ever hold it from the world apart,
Immured it lies among the meadows deep,
Its flowery stillness beautiful and calm as softest
sleep.   *John Russell Hayes*

It's hard to realize that this small Cornish manor was on the Domesday List, recorded in 1086. It was owned then by the half brother of William the Conqueror. Today, fine antiques, comfortable seating, lovely colors, fresh flowers, and log fires in winter combine to create an atmosphere of warmth and refinement. We admired handmade bargello covering some window-seat cushions.

Think of the nameless generations who have lived in this farmhouse and tilled these acres. In the rooms where you'll sleep, people in different dress were sleeping a hundred, two hundred, three hundred years ago. Could they have imagined such comforts as electric blankets and shiny modern bathrooms, one for each bedroom? Medieval times are suggested by the stone walls of the dining room. Guests sit together at one table to savor home cooking beautifully served. The reader who suggested we visit Manor Farm wrote, "My wife, a sometimes food critic, thought the cooking the best we had in twenty-one days in England."

A mile from the beach, Manor Farm is surrounded by gardens—camellias bloom in February—and 180 acres of mixed farming. The word fantastic is overused, but it truly applies to the price charged by the Knights.

Proprietors: Muriel and Paul Knight. *Recreational facilities:* Ocean swimming, surfing, sea-fishing, tennis, and riding nearby. *Other facilities:* Living room, games room, laundry, garden. *Rooms:* 4 with bath. Not suitable for children. Very inexpensive. Guests are asked not to smoke in the house. *How to get there:* At the junction of Route A39 and Route 3263, take a third road marked Crackington Haven. Pass the post office on the left. At the telephone booth, take a right, then the first right again. Pass one crossroad and find Manor Farm on the left, about 2 miles from Route A39. *Telephone:* (08403) 304.

Cranbrook, Kent

KENNEL HOLT

> English country life seemed to me the most advantageous
> thing in the world.
>
> *Henry James,* 1877

For pure country-house atmosphere, you'll go a long way to find anything to equal Kennel Holt. Its lounge is a spacious beamed and paneled library that invites evenings of conversation beside a fire. The handhewn beams of the house were put in place in 1588. Under them are wall-to-wall carpets, comfortable couches, books, and antiques. Every window at the inn has a different view of glorious gardens. Tea is served on the lawn. Mr. Cliff is a retired RAF wing commander; Mrs. Cliff has taught Cordon Bleu cooking for many years.

The house is set among England's greatest concentration of gardens and stately homes open to view. Just two and a half miles away is Sissinghurst, perhaps the most beautiful garden in England.

Proprietors: Mr. and Mrs. P.D. Cliff. *Closed:* December 24 through January. *Special facilities:* Lounge, sitting room, garden. *Rooms:* 7 with bath and TV. Moderate. *How to get there:* The hotel is signposted on Route A262, 2 miles northwest of Cranbrook. Do not go into the village. *Telephone:* (0580) 712032.

WILD BOAR HOTEL

> One bright unruffled evening must, if possible, be set
> apart for the splendour, the stillness, the solemnity of a
> three hours' voyage on the lake.
>> *William Wordsworth,* 1835

The Wild Boar is a country hotel but not a "country-house" hotel. The atmosphere is that of a professional hotel but one that is full of warmth and hospitality. Part of the building dates back to 1600, and there is a legend that the last boar of Westmorland was killed there.

Traditional red carpeting and red lampshades set off the white plaster walls and low black beams. Open fires in stone fireplaces welcome guests to cozy groupings of cretonne-covered chairs around black oak tables and tavern stools. Here and there are old high-backed settles and Flemish caned chairs. The bedrooms in the newest wing are attractively decorated in modern style, and some have balconies that offer splendid views of the moors and mountains of Cumbria.

The restaurant presents a large choice of excellent food and a fine selection of wines. Lake Windermere, one of England's premier resort areas, offers swimming and boating just a few miles away. This hotel will satisfy a fussy traveler.

Manager: Douglas Dale. *Recreational facilities:* Lake swimming, indoor pool, sauna, golf, riding, hunting, trout fishing, and rough shooting a short drive away. *Facilities for children:* Baby-sitting and -listening. *Other facilities:* Lounge, TV lounge, cocktail bar, garden. *Rooms:* 38 with bath, TV, telephone, tea-making. Ground floor rooms. Off-season rates; winter breaks; 3- or 4-day Christmas and New Year packages; children under 15 free if sharing. Moderate. *Restaurant service:* Luncheon, early and late snacks, tea, supper, dinner. *Credit cards:* Amex, Diners, Master, Visa. *How to get there:* Take exit 36 off superhighway M6. Follow the sign at the end of Kendal bypass marked "Hawkshead via ferry." The hotel is on the right 4 miles along on Route B5284. *Telephone:* (09662) 5225.   [T]

CROSBY LODGE

> The first near glance at this delighted us, for it was mani-
> fest that we had come upon a magnificent specimen of
> architecture of the bygone days when men built for them-
> selves grand habitations—the lordly few of the land, that
> is.
>
> *James Hissey, 1889*

A relaxed country-house atmosphere prevails at this crenallated, towered, and turreted mock castle secluded in the quiet of the Border
country. Ivy covers its walls, and cattle graze in its fields. There are open
fires surrounded with leather-topped fire fenders, Victorian tufted sofas,
and rose-patterned chintz. Room 6 features an Edwardian suite. Other
bedrooms are in traditional style, one with a tester bed, but a few have
simple modern furniture. Two bedrooms in a converted stable overlook a
walled garden.

Before dinner you'll enjoy drinks in a commodious bar with green velvet banquettes. Michael Sedgwick is his own chef, which insures that the
food is consistently delicious. Starters might be duck pâté with orange
salad, Stilton croquettes, or avocado mousse with prawns. A loin of veal
with Calvados and mushroom sauce was on one menu, as was roast duckling with orange sauce. A choice from a cheese board or desserts from a
trolley are followed by petits fours and coffee.

A dip into Scotland would be a fine day's outing for those who
haven't time to tour that land of bagpipes and heather.

Proprietors: Michael and Patricia Sedgwick. *Closed:* December
24—late January. *Facilities:* Lounge, TV room, cocktail bar, garden.
Rooms: 11 with bath and TV. Weekend breaks off season; discount for
children under 12. Moderate. *Restaurant service:* Luncheon, snacks, dinner. *Credit cards:* Amex, Diners. *How to get there:* The hotel is on B6264,
4 miles east of Carlisle. From M6, take exit 44 and follow the signs for
Brampton. *Telephone:* (0228 73) 618.

THE DEDHAM VALE HOTEL

A comfortable house is a great source of happiness.
Sydney Smith, 1843

The Dedham Vale is not only comfortable, it is beautiful. This country-house hotel was acquired a few years ago by the owner of the luxurious Maison Talbooth and the well-known Le Talbooth restaurant. Located between the two of them, it stands on terraced lawns amidst gardens of cultivated beauty. Bedrooms are decorated with sophistication to the same glamourous standard as those of Maison Talbooth, but they are a bit smaller and less expensive.

The Terrace Restaurant, of Edwardian-style glass reminiscent of the 1851 Crystal Palace, was added to the original Regency building. Its sunny colors, greenery, and flowers echo the gardens outside its windows. Featured is an elaborate black and brass French rotisserie in a green-tiled alcove on which steaks, kebobs, game, legs of lamb, and home-grown chickens are grilled. Among items on the menu are vegetarian specialities and desserts served from trolleys. For a change, guests can walk to the riverside Le Talbooth for meals.

Proprietor: Gerald Milsom. *Recreational facilities:* Riding, golf, tennis, and squash nearby. *Other facilities:* Lounge, cocktail bar, garden. *Rooms:* 6 with bath, telephone, and TV. Moderate to expensive. *Restaurant service:* Luncheon (except Saturday), dinner. *Credit cards:* Amex, Diners, Master, Visa. *How to get there:* Dedham is 7 miles north of Colchester, off Route A12. The hotel is on Stratford Road, 1 mile south of the village center, where you should ask directions. *Telephone:* (0206) 322273.   [T]

MAISON TALBOOTH

These scenes made me a painter.

John Constable

The Vale of Dedham is known throughout the world from the paintings of Constable, who immortalized the views you will see from your windows. Maison Talbooth has been decorated by a top London designer, who combined many antiques with modern touches such as a little bar in each bedroom, where peanuts and ice are placed at six each evening. It has been said that for each of the glamorous bathrooms there is a glamorous bedroom. Some tubs are round and others sunken. Despite all the luxury, this is a warm and friendly hotel, where guests meet as at a private house party.

A Continental breakfast is served, and a light sandwich lunch may be had in the charming living room or in the garden beyond the French doors. For other meals guests go to Le Talbooth, a celebrated restaurant half a mile away, or to the Dedham Vale Hotel, just down the road. Gerald Milsom developed his country-house hotel, Maison Talbooth,

after his restaurant, Le Talbooth, was already famous. Its ancient half-timber work of closely set studs filled with wattle and daub was painted by Constable. That painting hangs in the National Gallery of Scotland, in Edinburgh, but a copy is on the wall of the restaurant's entrance hall. The name Le Talbooth derives from the time when tolls were collected at a bridge crossing the River Stour, which flows beside the gardens where you may sit and sip a before-dinner drink. The restaurant has a fine wine list.

Manager: Jenny Paton Philip. *Recreational facilities:* Riding, golf, tennis, and squash a short drive away. *Other facilities:* Drawing room, garden. *Rooms:* 10 with bath, TV, and telephone. Suitable for wheelchair guests. Expensive to very expensive. *Restaurant service:* Luncheon, dinner (at Le Talbooth). *Credit cards:* Amex, Diners, Master, Visa. *How to get there:* Dedham is 7 miles north of Colchester, off Route A12. The hotel is on Stratford Road, 1 mile south of the village center, where you should ask directions. *Telephone:* (0206) 322367. *Agent in the United States:* Abercrombie and Kent. [T]

Diddlebury, Shropshire

GLEBE FARM

Sheltered, when the rain blew over the hill it was,
Sunny all day when the days of summer were long,
Beyond all rumour of laboring towns it was,
But at dawn and evening its trees were noisy with
song.

J.C. Squire, 1914

To be at Glebe Farm is to be in the sixteenth century, nicely modernized
for today's travelers. Michael Wilkes farmed 123 acres here for many years,
raising cattle, sheep, and poultry. In order to stay in their Tudor home when
he retired, the Wilkes turned it into a guest house.

One room has become a small cocktail bar where Michael presides before
dinner. He is a lively host who likes to mingle with his guests, encouraging

a congenial atmosphere. After dinner he joined us in the living room, telling us about life in this prosperous farming country. The room's plaster walls, with black beams embedded, were built by an old method called wattle and daub. Velvet draperies, a grand piano, a slant-top desk, various antiques, and shelves of books about gardening and silver convey an air of refinement and good taste.

The kitchen is the baliwick of Mrs. Wilkes, and her fine cooking is in keeping with the house. Beef, lamb, duck, and poultry are all produced on the home farm, which has been taken over by a son. So are milk, cream, butter, eggs, and vegetables. Make a dinner reservation when you book a room. The Wilkes take a few nonresidents for dinner when they have space. If you arrive unexpected late in the afternoon, they might have a bedroom for you but not a table for dinner. Everyone sits at separate tables at one time in a flagstoned, heavily beamed dining room that dates from 1580. The view from its windows is across the garden to a Saxon church with a forti-fied tower for which Glebe Farm was once the rectory. The Wilkes built an annex next to the house to provide four more bedrooms, including the only one with a private bath. We prefer to stay with the old, delighting in floors that slant and doorways through which we must duck.

A short walk from the house takes you to the foot of Wenlock Edge, made famous by A.E. Houseman's poem "A Shropshire Lad." This beautiful part of England near the Welsh border does not attract large numbers of tourists. In high season it would be a more enjoyable region to tour than the thronged roads of the southwest or the lake district.

Proprietors: Eileen and Michael Wilkes. *Closed:* Early November through February. *Recreational facilities:* Riding nearby. *Other facilities:* Living room, cocktail bar, garden. *Rooms:* 8, 1 with bath, all with tea-making. No children under 10. Inexpensive. *Restaurant service:* Dinner by reservation. *How to get there:* From Route A49 between Shrewsbury and Ludlow, take Route B4368 5 miles to Diddlebury. At the telephone booth, turn right to Glebe Farm. *Telephone:* (058476) 221.

Dorchester-on-Thames, Oxfordshire

THE GEORGE

Those towns that we call thorowfaires have sumptuous innes builded for the receiving of such travellers and strangers as passe to and fro...Everie man may have for his monie how great or how little varietie of vittels himself shall think expedient...if his chamber be once appointed he may carrie the kei with him so long as he lodgeth there.

William Harrison, 1563

The George was one of the "sumptuous innes" receiving strangers in 1563. It is believed to have been built to accommodate visitors to a twelfth-century Augustinian priory. Its overhanging gables, whitewashed walls, and mellow brickwork, its exposed beams and open log fires, are as warm and inviting today as they were to the long-ago travelers.

In the high-raftered dining hall, thought to be the original monks' brewhouse and one of the best examples of medieval domestic architecture left in England, you'll dine on food fresh from local farms and the hotel's garden. Some memorable wines are stored deep in the old cellars, and a selection of real ale is to be found in the tavern.

We first stopped here for lunch quite a few years ago and were charmed with the building. Now, different owners have since renovated The George, and it boasts twentieth-century comforts. For an appointment with the past, stay for a night and ask for a room with a four-poster bed.

Manager: Paul Dean. *Recreational facilities:* Outdoor and indoor pools, tennis, squash, boat hire, and boat trips nearby. *Other facilities:* TV lounge, public bar, garden. *Rooms:* 18, 16 with bath, all with telephone, TV, and tea-making. Ground-floor rooms, 2- or 3-day weekend reduction. Moderate. *Restaurant service:* Luncheon, snacks, dinner. *How to get there:* The inn is on Route A423 in the village. Guests can be met at Heathrow airport or at the train station in Didcot or Oxford. *Telephone:* (0865) 340404. [T]

East Grinstead, West Sussex

GRAVETYE MANOR

Of all the things that the English have invented . . . the most perfect, the most characteristic, the only one they have mastered . . . so that it becomes a compendious illustration of their social genius and their manners, is the well-appointed, well-ministered, well-filled country house.

Henry James, 1905

Both within and without, this place is beautiful. Wood fires burn fragrantly; guests meet in the paneled bar; the staff is solicitous and friendly; the wine cellar is one of the best in England; such dishes as hare and venison appear on the menu, along with Continental and English cuisine. Gravetye Manor is one of the most luxurious country-house hotels in Britain, distinguished but not stuffy.

The manor was built in 1598. Its most notable owner was William Robinson, one of the greatest gardeners of all time and author of *The English Flower Garden*. He bought the manor, and the 1,000 acres in which it stands, in 1884. Here he realized his idea of creating an English natural garden, now admired and copied all over the world. He paneled many of the rooms with oak from his woods, and today each bedroom is named for a different tree he planted — Ash, Birch, Beech, Holly.

In an earlier century the manor was used as a smugglers' hideout where plunder was distributed. Part of Smuggler's Lane still trails through the estate, which is a bird sanctuary. Gravetye Manor captures the spirit of English country-house hospitality. It is just a short drive from Gatwick Airport and is one of the few English members of the Relais et Chateaux Hotels, an association of renowned privately owned country hotels.

Proprietor: Peter Herbert. *Recreational facilities:* Tennis, squash, and riding a short drive away. *Rooms:* 14 with bath, TV, and telephone. 2-day advance reservation required for weekends. No children under 7. Expensive to very expensive. *Restaurant service:* Luncheon, dinner. *How to get there:* Signs for Gravetye Manor are on Route B2110 west of East Grinstead village and on B2028 coming from Brighton. The hotel will arrange for guests to be met at Gatwick Airport and put guests on a train for London at Three Bridges Station a day or two later, or the reverse if you are flying out of Gatwick. *Telephone:* (0342) 810567. *Agent in the United States:* David Mitchell. [T]

SUMMER LODGE

> She dipped down a hill...into the small town or village
> of Evershead...she made a halt there and breakfasted
> a second time...at a cottage by the church.
> *Thomas Hardy,* 1891

The thatched cottage where Tess had her breakfast is still by the church in Evershot, the Evershead of Thomas Hardy's *Tess of the D'Ubervilles*. Just down the road is the fine country-house hotel called Summer Lodge. Locally it is said that the illustrious author, who was a qualified architect, drew the plans for one wing of the hotel.

Nigel and Margaret Corbett escaped London to create this country house with a relaxed and informal atmosphere. Care, comfort, and courtesy are the keynotes. Nigel, who was working in the garden, greeted us cheerfully and took our bags as we walked from the parking area. We were soon enjoying afternoon tea with homemade shortbread before a fire.

The lounge is a gracious room, light and sunny, with plump chairs on which to read in comfort the magazines and books about Dorset that are on hand on antique tables. Bedrooms are pretty and comfortable, with views over gardens and fields.

The Corbetts' five-course dinner is commended in food guides. If you cannot eat certain things, or wish a vegetarian dinner, discuss the menu of the day with them. The wine list is above-average.

Summer Lodge is a hospitable place of quiet character that guests return to again and again.

Proprietors: Margaret and Nigel Corbett. *Closed:* December and January. *Recreational facilities:* Tennis and outdoor pool at the house; riding and golf nearby. *Other facilities:* Drawing room, TV room, cocktail bar, garden. *Rooms:* 9 with bath, telephone, and tea-making. Off-season breaks. No childen under 8. Expensive. *Restaurant service:* Dinner by reservation. *Credit cards:* Master, Visa. *How to get there:* Evershot is west off Route A37 at the village of Batcombe, between Dorchester and Yeovil. *Telephone:* (093583) 424.

THE COURT

My heart is warm with the friends I make,
And better friends I'll not be knowing...
Edna St. Vincent Millay

At this delightful home you'll really feel as if you are visiting friends. A reader suggested we see it, saying it was her favorite stop of a six-week trip, even though she stayed in some well-known luxurious country-house hotels. She became friends with the proprietors and planned to return and stay with them again.

The house is unique in that it dates back only to 1933 but was constructed of materials from an old mansion that was pulled down on the property. A splendid oak staircase was saved intact. We enjoyed sitting before a fire in a large, comfortable living room furnished with antiques. The sunny dining room, with blue and white plates displayed in a cabinet, looks onto a heather garden. Ask to see the secret door hidden in a bookcase.

Bedrooms are large, and although none have private baths there are plenty of bathrooms, some with showers, which is by no means common in English houses. Two of the five bedrooms are singles (at no supplementary charge). Dinner is a set meal, but changes can be made if the menu offers something you do not like. Fruits, vegetables, and milk from a Jersey herd are right from the 60 acres, which include river and woodland walks, a rock garden, and a pond. The Court is an informal place where people talk to each other. It gives wonderful value for your money.

Proprietors: Peggy Lazenby and Maureen Stevens. *Closed:* Mid-October to Easter. *Recreational facilities:* Golf nearby. *Other facilities:* Living room, garden. *Rooms:* 5 sharing baths, with tea-making. Very inexpensive. *How to get there:* From Route A356 in Frampton, northwest of Dorchester, take Southover Street across the River Frome. Then take the first left and find The Court on your left. *Telephone:* (0300) 20242.

Giggleswick, North Yorkshire

WOODLANDS

Tired with the town and all its noisy sway,
With eager haste I make the northern way,
Leave pomp and vanity, fatigue and care,
For sweet tranquility with rural fare.

Thomas Maude, 1771

Woodlands is a warm guest house with an air of friendly comfort. The Georgian house, once the center of an estate, is sited to take advantage of views across the Ribble valley, where sheep graze on grassy fields crisscrossed by stone walls. Here and there is a little stone farmhouse and byre tucked into a fold in the dales.

Welcoming bedrooms are named for trees that surround Woodlands —Hawthorn, Holly, Laurel, Silver Birch. All beds have continental quilts, and there is no supplement for a single room. The food, always fresh and with generous helpings, is especially good here: Roger Callan is a professional who lectures at a catering school. Thoughtful extras include early morning tea brought to your room with a newspaper. Margaret Callan brings late evening tea and coffee to the lounge, an attractive room with green velvet upholstery.

The village of Giggleswick is mentioned in the Domesday Book. In bustling Settle across the river, the open market is held every Tuesday. This highly recommended guest house is a good center for exploring both the Yorkshire dales and the Cumbrian lakes.

Proprietors: Margaret and Roger Callan. *Closed:* Christmas and New Year's Day. *Recreational facilities:* Indoor pool and squash a short walk away; tennis a short drive away. *Other facilities:* Living room, TV lounge, garden. *Rooms:* 10 sharing baths; TV available. Ground-floor rooms. Winter breaks. Reduction for children sharing. No children under 12. Inexpensive. *How to get there:* Woodlands is at the end of a cul-de-sac, signposted "The Mains" on Route A65, opposite the sign for Giggleswick. *Telephone:* (072 92) 2576.

COMBE HOUSE

> I dislike feeling at home when I'm abroad.
> *George Bernard Shaw*

You won't feel at home in Combe House—not unless home is just slightly less opulent than Blenheim Palace. Magnificent is the word for this Elizabethan mansion set in a beautiful estate. Grand as it is, however, it isn't intimidating. There's a "house-party" feeling to the place. Guests, staff, and owners mingle cordially.

Antique lovers will enjoy the fine architecture—ornate plasterwork ceilings, rococo fireplaces, rich paneling set off by vivacious colors as well as the furniture and paintings, many of them brought from the ancestral Boswell home, Auchinleck House, in Scotland. John Boswell is a direct descendant of *the* Boswell, of Boswell and Johnson fame.

In the Great Hall, guests sink into deep couches and chairs covered in lovely English floral fabrics, mostly grouped around a roaring fire. Enjoying a traditional Devon cream tea here, after a brisk walk to view the rhododendron, magnolia, and solid old trees on the extensive grounds, made us wonder if we hadn't stepped back into a Victorian novel. Bedrooms are spacious, with comfortable upholstered chairs.

Therese Boswell is French. She attended the Cordon Bleu school and runs the kitchen with the help of a team of Cordon Bleu cooks. The cuisine is French in inspiration, using the best of local fish, meat, and vegetables, some right from the estate gardens.

Gittisham is a showpiece little village of pale stone houses, thatched cottages, and a tiny towered church, all of which now belong to the National

Proprietors: John and Therese Boswell. *Recreational facilities:* Riding on the estate; outdoor pool, ocean swimming, tennis, squash, golf, boat rental, boat trips, sea-fishing, and hunting nearby. *Facilities for children:* Baby-sitting, children's supper. *Other facilities:* Hall lounge, drawing room, cocktail lounge, laundry service, garden. *Rooms:* 12 with bath, telephone, and TV; 1 suite. Winter breaks; 4-day Christmas program. Moderate to expensive. *Credit cards:* Amex, Diners, Master, Visa. *How to get there:* The house is signposted just south of Honiton on Route A30, the main London-to-Exeter road. *Telephone:* (0404) 2756. *Agent in the United States:* Abercrombie and Kent.

Goudhurst, Kent

STAR AND EAGLE

We were disposed to sleep under the very oldest English
architecture . . . we would be shown by delightfully narrow, crooked, and every way possible inconvenient stairways . . . into long, steep-roofed rooms.
Frederick Law Olmsted, 1850

The Tabard Inn, from which Chaucer's pilgrims began their journey into
Kent, vanished long ago, but the Star and Eagle was its contemporary;
those pilgrims might have stopped here. The narrow, crooked stairways
are in every way inconvenient, especially when one is carrying luggage.
The roughhewn beams and low-linteled doorways were put in place by
medieval craftsmen six hundred years ago, when people were much
shorter than they are today. Anyone over 5 feet tall must take great care,
as he wends his way to bed through tortuous passages, that he doesn't

give his head a jolly good crump, as they say in England. To experience such antiquity makes any necessary contortions worthwhile.

Bedrooms are bright and comfortable, fully carpeted, and with new furniture except for one bedroom with a four-poster. Fine bathrooms, some with oak beams embedded in walls, are new too. Everything is fresh —the antiquity does not include mustiness. The restaurant is very busy, with many patrons from the area. Medallions of veal in sherry or sirloin steak in brandy sauce are among extensive offerings that include traditional grills and roasts. Start with Smugglers' Grapefruit, segments steeped in dark rum, brown sugar, and ginger and served hot; end with a homemade dessert from the selection on a sideboard.

In the public bar is an inglenook fireplace with a nook to warm a tankard of beer. Villagers play darts and dominoes. The village has seen little change in four hundred years. The inn was headquarters for the Goudhurst Gang, eighteenth-century desperadoes. These smugglers and robbers terrorized the district until the village formed a militia to resist them. A pitched battle was fought, and the gang leader was shot in what is now the inn's parking lot. Tunnels led to both the historic Saint Mary's church next to the inn and the local manor house, Pattendene, which tells something of who protected the smugglers.

This aged inn in this ancient village is no archaic museum piece. Travelers in centuries past, in different dress, with different customs, have sat before its fires from feudal times to the present. History lives on at the Star and Eagle.

Manager: Christopher Satchell. *Closed:* A few days for Christmas. *Recreational facilities:* Indoor pool and riding nearby. *Facilities:* Lounge, cocktail bar, public bar, garden. *Rooms:* 11, 9 with bath, all with TV and tea-making. Breaks; reduction for children under 16 sharing (under 2 free). Inexpensive to moderate. *Restaurant service:* Luncheon, early and late snacks, dinner. *Credit cards:* Amex, Diners, Master, Visa. *How to get there:* Goudhurst is on Route A262, a few miles east of Royal Tunbridge Wells. *Telephone:* (0580) 211512.

Grasmere, Cumbria

MICHAELS NOOK

Upon the forest-side at Grasmere Vale
There dwelt a Shepherd, Michael was his name.
William Wordsworth

The name of this hotel salutes the memory of the shepherd Michael, whose cottage-dwelling was on this very site. A collector of fine antiques, Reginald Gifford runs Michaels Nook in a manner that conveys the atmosphere of an elegant home. There is no reception desk. Immediate impressions are of fireglow, gleaming silver, and rich old mahogany. Porcelain foot baths, old copper pans, and other such objects are imaginatively used as cachepots for fresh flowers and plants. A beautiful staircase sweeps upstairs, where some of the furniture was designed at the same time as the house to match the bedroom chimneypieces. In the dining room the china is Coalport, the crystal is Stuart, the silver is sterling, and the prices are high. The food, consistently praised by leading restaurant guides, was written up in *Gourmet* magazine. All guests book for dinner, bed, and breakfast.

Tables show off collections under glass, and Victorian domes protect gilt clocks. Anyone who likes to browse through antique shops will adore this place. Mr. Gifford has another hotel, the Wordsworth, in the center of Grasmere village. Renovation of the old place took eighteen months. Delicate plasterwork was restored, and many antiques are among the furnishings. With thirty-six bedrooms, an indoor heated pool, a sauna, and a solarium, it is more impersonal than Michaels Nook. The price is about the same, and most credit cards are accepted.

Proprietor: Reginald Gifford. *Recreational facilities:* Lake swimming, indoor pool, and sauna a short drive away. *Rooms:* 9 with bath, TV, and telephone; 2 suites. 4-day Christmas program. No children under 13. Expensive to very expensive. *Restaurant service:* Luncheon and dinner (by reservation). *How to get there:* Find the Swan hotel on Route A591. Turn uphill beside it and drive right into Michaels Nook. Avoid the Grasmere village center. *Telephone:* (09665) 496. *Agent in the United States:* Abercrombie and Kent.   [T]

WHITE MOSS HOUSE

> There was a quiet splendor, almost grandeur, about Grasmere vale . . . a kind of monumental beauty and dignity that agreed well with one's conception of the loftier strain of its poet.
>
> *John Burroughs,* 1884

White Moss House has beauty and dignity too, though it is not monumental. The house belonged to Wordsworth, although the poet never lived in it, and today it is an unusual hotel whose perfection of detail in both food and service has earned it renown.

There are only five bedrooms in the main house. Each offers books, magazines, a map of the Lake District, shoe cleaners, notepaper, a

sewing kit, a hair dryer, and fresh flowers, and each is furnished with an assortment of antiques mixed with necessary newer things. The Dixons have an extensive knowledge of the area and a great love for it. They will advise you on how best to spend a short or long stay, and particularly recommend some fell walking, a very popular British pastime.

Peter Dixon is in charge of all the cooking, which *Gourmet* magazine called outstanding. Everyone sits down to dinner at 8:00, and there is no choice of main course. Leg of Lakeland lamb, roast Coniston duckling, and poached Solway salmon are some of the entrées offered on different nights. There is a choice of three or four desserts that might include apricot brandy flan, raspberry shortcake, homemade raisin and rum ice cream, Westmorland raisin and nut pie with rum cream. English cheeses with White Moss oat biscuits, then coffee and mints, follow the desserts. All bookings are for dinner, as well as bed and breakfast.

In addition to the rooms in the main house, there is Brockstone cottage, a short drive or an "energetic" walk away, with living room and two bedrooms. This pleasant hotel, with a tradition of personal service, is for quiet people who will enjoy talking with the other guests in a homelike atmosphere.

Proprietors: Sue and Peter Dixon. *Closed:* November to mid-March. *Recreational facilities:* Tennis, squash, riding, lake and river swimming, and an indoor pool a short drive away. *Other facilities:* Lounge, garden. *Rooms:* 5 with bath and a 2-bedroom cottage with bath. 3-day minimum advance reservation. 3-day reduction. Not suitable for children. Expensive. *Restaurant service:* Dinner by reservation. *How to get there:* The hotel is on Route A591 between Ambleside and Grasmere. *Telephone:* (096 65) 295.

SWAN

Who does not know the famous Swan?
William Wordsworth, 1819

A roadside inn immortalized by Wordsworth in his poem "The Waggoner," this old hostelry, which was established about three hundred years ago, has retained its hospitable character over the centuries.

The beamed lounge, with a chair that belonged to the great poet himself and warmed with old oaken furniture displaying antique china, says, "Welcome," as does the informal garden. The bedrooms are mostly modern.

In 1854 Hawthorne wrote, "I . . . passed the Swan inn, where Scott used to go daily and get a draught of liquor, when he was visiting Wordsworth, who had no wine or other inspiriting fluid in his house."

Manager: Peter Coward. *Recreational facilities:* Lake swimming, sauna; and indoor pool nearby. *Other facilities:* Lounge, TV lounge, public bar, garden. *Rooms:* 41, 25 with bath. Reduction for children under 14 sharing (under 5 free); winter breaks; Christmas program. Moderate. *Restaurant service:* Luncheon, snacks, tea, dinner. *Credit cards:* Amex, Carte Blanche, Diners, Master, Visa. *How to get there:* The hotel is on Route A591 in Grasmere. *Telephone:* (09665) 551. *Agent in the United States:* THF.

[T]

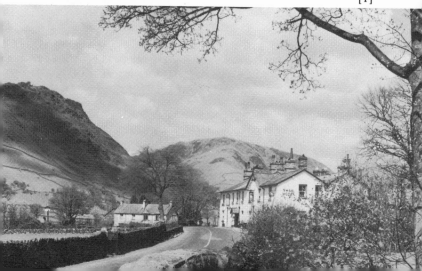

LANGDALES HOTEL

> I don't talk much about these things, but these lakes and
> mountains give me a deep joy for which I suspect nothing
> else can compensate.
>
> *Robert Southey,* 1821

Poet Laureate Robert Southey testifies to the beauty of the Cumbrian mountains that surround Langdales Hotel. The Farrars will make you welcome right away in this secluded spot. If you are tired of sight-seeing, this would be a restful place to take a few days off. Read in the gardens that run down to a river. They hold appealing lawn furniture. Inside, curl up before a fire on cool days. Ask for a packed lunch to take onto the fells and pick blackberries along the way.

Bedrooms are simply furnished with pretty color schemes, and there is no supplement for a single room. Homemade scones come with afternoon tea, and rolls and pastries are homemade too. Local venison is featured in season, and the White Lion Bar is a popular local meeting place.

Although Langdales is secluded, it is not too far off the beaten track to be a good center for visiting all of the Lake District. Peter O'Toole has been a guest here.

Proprietors: Anne and Ken Farrar. *Recreational facilities:* Lake and river swimming and trout fishing at the hotel; tennis, squash, riding, boat rental, and boat trips nearby. *Facilities for children:* Baby-listening. *Other facilities:* Lounge, TV lounge, cocktail bar, garden. *Rooms:* 20, 16 with bath. Winter breaks. Reduction for children sharing; Christmas and New Year's program. Moderate. *Restaurant service:* Early and late snacks, tea, dinner. *How to get there:* From Route A593, between Coniston and Ambleside, take Route B5343 to Langdales Hotel. *Telephone:* (096 67) 253.

Greta Bridge, North Yorkshire

MORRITT ARMS

To our great joy we discovered a comfortable room, with
drawn curtains, and a most blazing fire. In half an hour
they gave us a smoking supper, and a bottle of mulled
port.

Charles Dickens

The great author wrote the words above to his wife from Greta Bridge
while he was at the George Inn, long gone. The Morritt Arms is dedicated
to the memory of Dickens and the George, and a right good job has been
made of it. The atmosphere of the dark-paneled public rooms, with
Jacobean furniture, firelight bouncing off a gleam of polished copper,
"ceilings heavy with massive beams," makes us think that Dickens's own
words were rightly used as a guide for the interior design: "a delicious
perspective of warmth and brightness — when the ruddy gleam of the fire
streaming through the old red curtains of the common room, seemed to
bring with it, as part of itself, a pleasant hum of voices, and a fragrant

odour of steaming grog and rare tobacco, all steeped, as it were, in the cheerful glow."

From here you can explore the haunting beauty of the lonely Yorkshire moors and dales. Sir Walter Scott called this countryside "one of the most enviable places I have ever seen." It is the setting for his famous *Rokeby*, dedicated to his friend John Morritt with the words "the scene of which is laid in his beautiful demesne of Rokeby." The Morritt Arms was named for the family of Scott's friend. Stop for lunch or tea if you don't stay overnight.

Manager: Rodney Waldron. *Recreational facilities:* Tennis and riding a short drive away. *Facilities for children:* Playground. *Other facilities:* Lounge, cocktail bar, public bar, garden. *Rooms:* 28, 13 with bath, all with TV. Suitable for wheelchair guests. Reduction; 2-day breaks; reduction for children sharing. Inexpensive to moderate. *Restaurant service:* Luncheon, snacks all day, tea, dinner. *Credit cards:* Diners, Master, Visa. *How to get there:* Greta Bridge is about 3 miles south of Barnard Castle on Route A66. *Telephone:* (0833) 27232. [T]

Grimsthorpe, Lincolnshire

BLACK HORSE INN

> The English wayside inn is a feature of the English countryside . . . at its best there is a cosiness and cheer about it which warm the heart, as its quaintness and savour of past days keep alive the sense of romantic travel.
> *Richard Le Gallienne,* 1915

The Black Horse Inn is a hostelry of individuality from its furnishings to its food, but its food is what it is famous for. Lauded in all restaurant guides, it specializes in the very best English cooking: a family member helps guests choose from the large menu; vegetables come from a garden across the road, freshly picked and cooked to order; herbs are from the inn's own herb garden: other items are from nearby farms. A memorable dinner might feature Elizabethan pork, deviled lamb kidneys with

brandy, or Mrs. Beeton's beafsteak, kidney, and mushroom pie. For luncheon you could try shepherd's pie or chicken livers Osbert Sitwell. Some desserts are from old recipes, some are original: honey meringues, treacle tart, or apple pie with cream. The sophisticated and charming Fishers, who own the Black Horse, have demonstrated their cooking on various TV stations during an American tour and have been featured on the BBC.

Your first welcome will be the warmth of a log fire. The decorating does justice to the food — stone walls, different kinds of antique tables, Adam firedogs, silver candelabra, chrysanthemums, gourds and pine cones arranged about stuffed pheasants. The bar has walls of natural plaster, black beams, and a red rug. There's old oak, a coal fire glowing on a stone hearth, a friendly black dog.

Bedrooms are small but thoroughly comfortable, pretty with floral chintz and fresh flowers. There is a nice single room with bath at the same rate per person as the doubles.

This Black Horse Inn is a special sort of place. It is unpretentious but very first class, with meticulous attention to detail. The duke and duchess of Gloucester have been guests. As might be expected, the food is expensive but value is received. The family will help plan your day trips, recommending the best places to shop. You can drive to nearby Peterborough and take a train into London for the day.

Proprietors: Kay and Joyce Fisher. *Closed:* Sundays and Christmas. *Recreational facilities:* Outdoor pool a short drive away. *Other facilities:* TV lounge, cocktail bar, garden. *Rooms:* 4 with bath and tea-making. 2-day minimum advance reservation. Moderate. *Restaurant service:* Luncheon, dinner. *Credit cards:* Amex, Master, Visa. *How to get there:* Grimsthorpe is on Route A151 between Bourne and Grantham. *Telephone:* (077 832) 247.

Hawkhurst, Kent

TUDOR ARMS

The County of Kent is rich in medows pastures and pleasant Groves, and wonderfully aboundeth with Apples and Cheeries.

Celia Fiennes, 1697

At this unpretentious, sunny inn in the weald of Kent, renowned as the garden of England, you will find a courteous welcome. The feature of the hotel is its exceptional garden, where meals are served under the trees when weather permits. The garden encompasses a glass house filled with flowers (masses of red geraniums when we visited), a putting green, and a playground with swings, and it's surrounded by hop fields.

Pretty floral draperies, plants, fresh flowers, books, magazines, a nice old desk, and a copper chestnut roaster give the lounge a pleasant, bright aspect, although the furniture is very plain. In the bar, the glow of a fire sets off nice old paneling, and a cabinet holds small gifts for sale. The dining room features some French and Italian dishes and uses fresh local produce; bedrooms are comfortably modern, bathrooms are almost new, and the whole place shines.

For those who prefer a base in the country from which to sightsee, we suggest a stay here. Some cities within easy reach are busy, crowded Canterbury, Eastbourne, the Cinque Ports of Sussex and Kent, and the port of Dover.

Manager: Karen Bradbury. *Recreational facilities:* Tennis at the hotel; riding and sauna nearby. *Facilities for children:* Baby-sitting; playground. *Other facilities:* Lounge, cocktail bar, public bar, garden. *Rooms:* 14, 6 with bath, TV available. Reductions, reduction for children sharing; Christmas program. Inexpensive to moderate. *Restaurant service:* Luncheon, early and late snacks, tea, dinner. *Credit cards:* Amex, Diners, Master, Visa. *How to get there:* The hotel is on Route A268, 1 mile from Hawkhurst on the road to Rye. *Telephone:* (058 05) 2312. *Agent in the United States:* Best Western.   [T]

Henley-on-Thames, Oxfordshire

HERNES

> An old English family mansion is a fertile subject for study. It abounds with illustrations of former times, and traces of the tastes, and humors, and manners, of successive generations.
>
> *Washington Irving,* 1822

For five generations, Hernes has been home to one English family. Surrounded by lawns, trees, and gardens, and with an outdoor heated swimming pool, the house, begun in the sixteenth century, is part of a 400-acre farm estate.

Gillian Ovey says she loves to entertain; and, to help pay for her children's education, she prefers entertaining paying guests to getting a conventional job. Gillian is warm and friendly. Upon our arrival she brought us afternoon tea and sat down for a chat. We were in a gracious, wood-paneled living room—one of those large entrance rooms so typical of old English houses and called The Hall. Chairs and sofa covered with brocade and velvet were grouped informally before a wide hearth where flames snapped. Brass firetools gleamed. Magazines and brochures of nearby attractions were on handsome old tables, along with fresh flowers in Chinese porcelain vases and bibelots collected by former generations. An ancestor portrait or two hung on the paneling, and a grand piano in one corner held framed family photographs. The room was welcoming.

Our spacious bedroom was the loveliest of our trip. In our bathroom, besides the usual fixtures, were a bidet, two antique mahogany chests of drawers, a cheval mirror, and, best of all, a fire going in a stove set into a former fireplace.

We knocked on the door at four o'clock without a reservation, but don't do the same. Call ahead so you can have dinner with the Oveys and savor home-produced meat and game, vegetables, milk, butter, and eggs from the farm. Gillian serves a four-course dinner, but you can ask for a light supper. Hernes is not licensed, but guests may bring their own drinks. Gillian told us she'd have been happy to fix a meal for us but Richard was holding a church-related meeting in their dining room that evening. When we returned from dinner, we relaxed again before the fire and met some of Richard's guests while we drank coffee Gillian brought in.

Henley-on-Thames is central to Windsor, Eton, Ascot, Wimbledon, Oxford, Bath, and storybook Cotswold villages. As it is only 35 minutes from Heathrow, a stay at Hernes would be a memorable introduction to England.

Proprietors: Gillian and Richard Ovey. *Recreational facilities:* Outdoor pool at the house; riding, boat rental, and boat trips on the Thames nearby. *Other facilities:* Living room, billiards room, garden. *Rooms:* 3 with bath. Not suitable for young children. Moderate. *How to get there:* From the bridge across the Thames River into Henley, go straight for a block and turn left onto Duke Street. Turn right onto Greys Road. Drive along this winding road until you reach the Indoor Sports Centre. Turn right and find Hernes about a mile along on the right. *Telephone:* (0491) 573245.

RED LION

Who'er has travelled life's dull round,
Where'er his stages may have been,
May sigh to think how oft he found
The warmest welcome at an inn.
William Shenstone, 1737

"We happened to lie this night at the inn at Henley, where Shenstone wrote these lines," said Boswell. Yes, this is the place where Shenstone is said to have scratched on a window pane what are probably the most familiar words written about inns.

The Red Lion, a storied inn, was given the name of Anglers Inn in Dickens's *Our Mutual Friend.* Charles I and George IV slept under its ancient timbers, and a room was always kept ready for the original Duke of Marlborough, for a break in his trip between London and Blenheim. Bedrooms are named for the famous historical characters who have visited this most renowned of old coaching inns: Queen Charlotte, Dr. Johnson, Prince Rupert.

Directly across the Thames from the famous rowing club, the Red Lion offers grandstand viewing of the Royal Henley Regatta, since 1839 the principal gathering of amateur oarsmen from all over the world. Ask for a room overlooking the river. We awakened our first morning in England to sunlight dancing on the ceiling, reflected from the famous waters. Crews in rowing shells were already at practice. This was *England,* no doubt about that.

Henley-on-Thames, a bustling town of about 12,000 not far from Heathrow Airport, is a wonderful place to start a tour of Britain. You will be quickly immersed in English life as you go in and out of stores, have afternoon tea in little tearooms, walk beside the Thames watching all the boat traffic, stop in pubs that cater to locals, not tourists. There are fine antique shops for browsing, but prices are high. If you want just a quick look at London, the trains run frequently, as many people commute.

The old red-brick facade of the Red Lion, mantled with wisteria and banked with flowers, has changed little over the centuries. Ashley Sterry wrote of it,

Tis a finely toned, picturesque, sunshiny, place,
Recalling a dozen old stories;
With a rare British, good-natured, ruddy-hued face,
Suggesting old wines and old Tories.

Although the Red Lion is well run and well maintained, we wish a good decorator would redo the whole interior to capture the coaching-inn atmosphere this famous old hotel should have.

Manager: Charles Ratcliff. *Recreational facilities:* Boat rental and boat trips on the Thames a short walk away. *Other facilities:* Lounge, cocktail bar, public bar. *Rooms:* 28, 18 with bath, all with TV and telephone. 2-day breaks. Moderate. *Restaurant service:* Luncheon, dinner. *Credit cards:* Amex, Visa. *How to get there:* The Red Lion is on Hart Street. Trains from London are frequent. *Telephone:* (0491) 572161. [T]

Horton-cum-Studley, Oxfordshire

STUDLEY PRIORY

> There are long corridors, an intricate arrangement of
> passages, and an up-and-down meandering of staircases,
> amid which it would be no marvel to encounter some
> forgotten guest who had gone astray a hundred years
> ago, and was still seeking for his bedroom while the rest
> of his generation were in their graves.
>
> *Nathaniel Hawthorne,* 1855

If Studley Priory looks familiar, you probably saw the movie *A Man for
All Seasons*, in which it portrays the home of Sir Thomas More. A
twelfth-century Benedictine convent turned into an Elizabethan manor
after the dissolution of the nunneries by Henry VIII, its woods were
ordered cut down by Cardinal Wolsey to build Christ Church at Oxford.
Studley Priory fits Hawthorne's description quoted above, but it was a
private home at the time Hawthorne lived in England.

We went through a network of passages, corridors, and stairs to reach
our room, thinking perhaps we should have unwound a ball of twine
behind us to find our way back. Our bedroom was attractively furnished,
though not with old things, and if you hope to get one appointed with
antiques, ask well ahead. You will pay a bit extra for the one with a
magnificent Elizabethan tester bed constructed from linenfold paneling.
Coats of arms of the Croke family, who owned Studley Priory for more
than three hundred years, line the cornice of the reception lounge. These
armorial bearings are repeated in stained glass in windows.

Only 7 miles from Oxford, this hotel makes a good country base from
which to explore the large, busy city. Some of you might enjoy the
special-interest weekends, for an all-inclusive fee that covers lectures on
such subjects as wine, antiques, and old books.

Manager: J. R. Parke. *Closed:* First 2 weeks of January. *Recreational
facilities:* Tennis at the hotel; trapshooting and squash a short drive away.
Other facilities: 2 lounges, cocktail bar, garden. *Rooms:* 19 with bath,
TV, telephone, and tea-making. Suitable for wheelchair guests. 2-day
breaks. Moderate to very expensive. *Restaurant service:* Luncheon, din-

ner. *Credit cards:* Amex, Carte Blanche, Diners, Master, Visa. *How to get there:* At the Headington rotary on Route A40, just northeast of Oxford, look for signs for Horton-cum-Studley (sometimes shown as just "Studley" on maps). *Telephone:* (086 735) 203. *Agent in the United States:* Romantik Hotels. [T]

Hovingham, North Yorkshire

WORSLEY ARMS

He goes not out of his way who goes to a good inn.
George Herbert, 1633

Cricket is the theme at the Worsley Arms, named for the family of the duchess of Kent, who are lords of the manor hereabouts. The duchess's father, Sir William, was captain of champion Yorkshire teams. Old photographs of famous cricketeers and old cricketing prints are displayed on the walls of one lounge, and the family arms enliven the inn sign in front of the golden stone building.

The hotel, built in the graceful Georgian period, has high ceilings and a light, airy feeling. Furnishings are a mix — some wicker among antiques and modern pieces. Food served in the attractive dining room is recommended in English restaurant guides. Roast pork with applesauce would have been our choice had we stayed for dinner. Starters included soused herring, chilled watercress soup, and cream of asparagus soup. Raspberry gateau would surely have been our dessert. Roomy bedrooms have matching floral wallpapers and draperies.

The Worsley Arms is not ye little olde rustic village inn. The atmosphere is refined, professional, and a bit reserved. Stop by for afternoon tea between 4:00 and 5:30 if you're in the neighborhood. This very civilized hotel will suit discriminating travelers.

Proprietors: Mr. and Mrs. Brian Precious. *Closed:* 2 days at Christmas. *Recreational facilities:* Tennis a short walk away; sauna and riding a short drive away. *Other facilities:* 2 lounges, TV lounge, cocktail bar, public bar, garden. *Rooms:* 14 with bath. 2-day reduction; reduction for children sharing. Moderate. *Restaurant service:* Luncheon, snacks, tea, dinner. *Credit cards:* Master, Visa. *How to get there:* The hotel is on Route B1257 in Hovingham, between York and Kirkbymoorside. *Telephone:* (065 382) 234.

HUNTSHAM COURT

> There are few hours in life more agreeable than the hour
> dedicated to the ceremony known as afternoon tea.
> *Henry James*

Many of the guests were gathered for tea in front of a fire in the Great Hall when we arrived. If you like hotels with a house-party atmosphere, don't miss this one. Huntsham Court is friendly, idiosyncratic, and fun.

It's a large sixteenth-century manor, remodeled in high Victorian style, a good setting for a Gothic suspense novel. Furniture is mostly old, but don't expect fine antiques; the atmosphere is casual rather than one of polished perfection. In the bar, help yourself and note what you took in a logbook. Visit the butler's pantry for light refreshments during the day. If the weather is inclement, work out in the mini-gym, suffer in the sauna, or gather a stack of books from the library shelves and sink into a chair. On good days take a house bicycle to pedal along leafy lanes and then return to lounge.

Huntsham Court is a place for music lovers. Over 2,000 recordings, mostly of classical works (along with a few with the big band sound), are in a music library. Guests can play their favorites on record players placed in the various lounges. Bedrooms are named for composers.

A dinner party takes place each evening. Guests are seated by placecard at one long, candlelit table. Your placecard will have not your own name but the name of the composer on your bedroom door. We were Mr. and Mrs. Beethoven. On my right sat Mr. Mozart, a geophysicist from Nova Scotia. To my left was Mr. Handel, a young businessman from London. Mrs. Handel, a lawyer, sat next to my husband. Couples are separated unless they ask to sit together, or unless the Bolwigs sense that they might be shy. Dressy clothes are not required; your traveling clothes will do fine, although men will be more comfortable in a coat and tie.

Proprietors: Andrea and Mogens Bolwigs. *Recreational facilities:* Bicycles, sauna, and mini-gym at the house; riding nearby. *Other facilities:* Great hall, drawing room, billiards room, library, music room, cocktail bar, laundry service, garden. *Rooms:* 12 with bath. Moderate to expensive. *Restaurant service:* Dinner by reservation. *Credit cards:* Master, Visa. *How to get there:* From Taunton take Route 361 towards Bampton. Follow signs to Huntsham Court. *Telephone:* (039860) 210. [T]

YE OLDE BELL

> By Hurley Weir . . . I have often thought that I could stay
> a month without having sufficient time to drink in all the
> beauty of the scene. The village of Hurley . . . is as old a
> little spot as there is on the river, dating from times of
> King Sebert and King Offa.
>
> *Jerome K. Jerome,* 1889

Ye Olde Bell, pictured on our cover, claims to be the oldest inn in England. In 1135 it began life as a guest house of a Benedictine monastery, and tradition has it that there still remains a walled underground passage to the monastery ruins. The Cavalier soldier-poet Richard Lovelace wrote some of his memorable poems while under its ancient beams. Beside a blazing fire in the great fireplace of the lounge bar are mementos of more recent history—framed letters from General Dwight Eisenhower and Winston Churchill, frequent visitors during World War II, when American officers were quartered in Hurley.

Our bedroom, furnished with antiques that included a Victorian sofa, had a dressing room and overlooked a garden filled with morning bird song. A few rooms have modern furnishings; so ask for the antiques. Some doorways off the twisting, narrow hallways are only 5 feet 6 inches high and bear placards that say "Duck or Grouse."

A five-minute walk through the little village brings you to a rural section of the Thames where boats and swans go through a lock every few minutes. The restaurant, with its exceptional food, attracts guests from London. On our last visit we were told Princess Anne had dined there recently and a member of the royal family had just booked rooms.

Manager: Patricia Wright. *Recreational facilities:* Golf at the hotel; squash a short walk away; riding a short drive away. *Other facilities:* Lounge, cocktail bar, public bar, garden. *Rooms:* 19 with bath, TV, and telephone. Moderate to expensive. *Restaurant service:* Luncheon, snacks, tea, dinner. *Credit cards:* Amex, Diners, Visa. *How to get there:* The inn is signposted on Route A423 between Henley and Maidenhead. *Telephone:* (062882) 4244. [T]

MEADOW HOUSE

Among the meadows of the countryside,
From city noise and tumult far away.
John Russell Hayes

David and Marion MacAuslan left all city noise and tumult far away when they departed London to entertain guests in this historic sixteenth-century rectory, set in eight acres of garden with a stream and waterfall. After we walked through the exceptionally attractive rooms, we were not surprised to learn that Marion had worked as an interior designer. The impression is light and airy—a quarry-tile entrance hall, stripped pine, floral fabrics, pretty colors. Bedrooms are large, with luxurious bathrooms and views of the Bristol Channel and the Quantocks.

Dining inside or on the garden terrace, guests may sit together or not, as they choose. The menu, which changes daily, combines imagination with culinary expertise and makes full use of garden and local produce. You may find some unusual items such as quail eggs. Choices of main course the day we arrived were breast of chicken poached in white wine with watercress sauce, fillet of lamb, and baked red mullet. David's hobby is wine, and over a hundred varieties stock his cellar. Smoking is not allowed except in a smoking lounge, once the rector's study.

We came upon Meadow House one morning after we had stayed at an ancient inn that had been modernized in a disappointing manner. How sorry we were that we had not gone just a little farther to find this delightful place.

Proprietors: David and Marion MacAuslan. *Recreational facilities:* Riding, ocean swimming, and golf nearby. *Facilities for children:* Childsitting. *Other facilities:* Lounge, smoking room, billiard room, cocktail bar, garden. *Rooms:* 4 with bath, TV, and tea-making; 2-bedroom self-catering cottage. 3-day reduction. No children under 9. Inexpensive. *Credit cards:* Master, Visa. *How to get there:* Kilve is signposted on Route 39 just east of Williton. *Telephone:* (027874) 546.

Kirkbymoorside, North Yorkshire

GEORGE AND DRAGON

No more the coaches shall I see
Come trundling from the yard,
Nor hear the horn blown cheerily
By brandy-bibbing guard.

Anonymous

On a quaint market square, the George and Dragon has provided hospitality since the thirteenth century. You'll drive under an arch into an innyard where coach wheels once clattered over cobblestones. The inn's homey atmosphere is fostered by Anne and Peter Curtis and their daughter and son-in-law, Sheila and Trevor Austin. One of them is always at hand to give personal service. They raise race horses, and some are stabled behind the inn.

We discovered the George and Dragon before lunch one morning—too early to settle in for the day. Having been disappointed with our two previous nights' lodgings, we found this inn appealing and mapped a circle tour to the coast that would bring us back to Kirkbymoorside for dinner and overnight. A fire welcomed us in a friendly beamed taproom where we talked with many English overnight guests and local residents. The dining room's imaginative menu provides a varied choice that caters to all tastes and budgets and offers a carefully selected wine list. Meticulous, well-appointed bedrooms have modern unit furniture and good modern bathrooms. From November to Easter (except for New Year's), the rate is a great bargain—just half price, providing you stay two days and take dinner. Really to mix with the British, book well ahead for the New Year's program, which features a festive dance on New Year's Eve. Some guests return yearly for it.

Proprietors: Anne and Peter Curtis, Sheila and Trevor Austin. *Closed:* 2 days at Christmas. *Recreational facilities:* Tennis and squash a short walk away; riding and hunting a short drive away. *Other facilities:* Lounge, public bar, garden. *Rooms:* 23, 20 with bath, all with TV. Suitable for wheelchair guests. 2-day breaks; New Year's program. Not suitable for children under 6. Inexpensive. *Restaurant service:* Luncheon, snacks, dinner. *Credit cards:* Master, Visa. *How to get there:* Kirkbymoorside is on Route A170 between Helmsley and Pickering. *Telephone:* (0751) 31637.

THE SIGN OF THE ANGEL

> It is one of those rich morsels of quaint antiquity which give such a peculiar character to the English landscape.
> *Washington Irving*, 1822

In a village so quaint and picturesque that it looks like a view on a Christmas card, the Sign of the Angel has a rare warmth and antiquity. This fourteenth-century house of great atmosphere, with period furnishings and fine paneling, is cared for with pride by the Levis family. Heavily beamed bedrooms come in odd shapes, with floors not always quite level and doors slightly askew—all assets to those who love ancient architecture.

The candlelit dining room, with open fire in a walk-in fireplace, provides a romantic setting for the gourmet cooking of Mrs. Levis and her daughter-in-law, Lorna. The main course is usually a roast with a garniture of colorful fresh vegetables. There is an inventive selection of appetizers, homebaked bread, and delectable desserts slathered with thick cream, followed by a fine Stilton. Reserve for dinner when you book your room, as diners come from miles around.

The whole village, with timber-framed cottages, some roofed with thatch, belongs to the National Trust, as does its thirteenth-century abbey and manor farm. It was given to the Trust by the Talbot family, whose most famous member was W. H. Fox-Talbot, a pioneer of photography who made the first photographic prints in 1833. An abbey barn houses the Kodak Photographic Museum.

This medieval village is a fine destination for train travelers, as the inn will send someone to meet the train at Chippenham at no charge. Jaunts about the countryside can be made by local bus. A stay here will be a memorable experience.

Proprietors: The Levis family. *Closed:* December 22—January 1. *Other facilities:* Lounge, garden. *Rooms:* 6 with bath. Off-season rates. No children under 12. Moderate. *Restaurant service:* Luncheon (closed Saturday), dinner (closed Sunday). *How to get there:* Lacock is on Route A350, 2 miles from Chippenham. Guests can be met at the Chippenham railway station. *Telephone:* (024 973) 230.

LAMORNA COVE HOTEL

> Is there not an inn at the Land's End where you can lie
> awake in a rest that is better than slumber, listening to the
> noise of the sea upon the Longships and to the Atlantic
> wind?
>
> *Hilaire Belloc, 1912*

Not far from Land's End, this old mansion, with a dining room that was
once a chapel, has been well furnished in modern style with some antique
accents. The gentle climate of South Cornwall provides flowers the year
round. From the stone-terraced swimming pool the banks of rhododendrons complement the vistas off to sea. A path beside a stream meanders
down steep, wooded slopes to a little quay on the strand below, where
once smugglers probably labored on stormy nights to unload their
contraband, for this is the country where the *Poldark* television series
was filmed. The marvelous public footpaths of England, which stretch
out across the granite cliffs along almost all of Cornwall's coastline, will
take you to the industrious little fishing port of Mousehole.

We met an American couple who came for one night but stayed at this
hotel the entire last week of their English vacation.

Proprietors: Mr. and Mrs. Bolton. *Closed:* December. *Recreational
facilities:* Outdoor pool, ocean swimming, and sauna at the hotel; tennis,
golf, riding, deep-sea fishing, surfing, and waterskiing a short drive
away. *Facilities for children:* Baby-sitting and -listening. *Other facilities:*
2 lounges, sun lounge, cocktail bar, garden. *Rooms:* 22 with bath,
telephone, and TV. Elevator. Off-season rates; 2-day breaks; reduction
for children sharing. Moderate to expensive. *Restaurant service:*
Luncheon, snacks, tea, supper, dinner. *Credit cards:* Amex, Diners,
Master, Visa. *How to get there:* The hotel is on the Channel coast south
of Penzance, where guests can be met at the railway station. Cars can be
rented nearby. *Telephone:* (0736) 731564.   [T]

Lavenham, Suffolk

SWAN HOTEL

> The Swan is a little masterpiece, the red of old gables
> tumbling to leaded lights, the cream of plaster, the brown
> of studs. It has the soft glow of an old Dutch painting.
> *Hammond Innes*

With its origins in the fourteenth century, the Swan ranks among the most perfect of half-timbered buildings in Great Britain and is a pride of the Trust House Forte Hotels, some of which have been modernized much less sensitively.

The spell of history hangs over the Swan, and a more recent chapter was added when American fliers stationed nearby during World War II left their names recorded on the walls of the bar. You reach your room through uneven, narrow passages—down a step here, walk uphill a bit, now down three steps, turn, oops! mind your head! But there is nothing historic about the sleek modern bathrooms.

The blue cloth of Lavenham was famous throughout Europe before Columbus set sail to find that new route to the Indies. Immensely rich merchants built the Wool Hall and Guildhall, which still remain, as does the perpendicular church, unique for the peal of its bells and its priceless carvings. Around the corner from the Swan, in the early nineteenth century, a Miss Jane Taylor wrote a simple little poem known throughout the English-speaking world—"Twinkle, Twinkle, Little Star."

In this commodious and busy inn, the atmosphere is impersonal—hotel-like. For those who love old buildings but must go first class all the way, the Swan is an excellent choice.

Manager: P.G. Manby. *Recreational facilities:* Tennis and riding a short walk away; golf a short drive away. *Facilities for children:* Baby-listening, children's menu. *Other facilities:* 2 lounges, cocktail bar, public bar, garden. *Rooms:* 42 with bath, TV, telephone, and tea-making. Ground-floor rooms. 2-day breaks; discount for children under 16 (free if sharing). Moderate. *Restaurant service:* Luncheon, snacks, tea, dinner. *Credit cards:* Amex, Carte Blanche, Diners, Master, Visa. *How to get there:* Lavenham is on Route A1141 northeast of Sudbury. *Telephone:* (0787) 247 477. *Agent in the United States:* THF. [T]

HOPE END

Gentle the land is, where my daily
Steps in jocund childhood played,
Dimpled close with hill and valley,
Dappled very close with shade.
Summer snow of apple blossom
Running up from glade to glade.

Elizabeth Barrett Browning

A romantic history has Hope End, whose most famous resident was Elizabeth Barrett Browning. The house in which she spent twenty-three years was demolished in 1873, but a few years ago, John and Patricia Hegarty, formerly a lawyer and a teacher, transformed the stables and coach houses into a unique small hotel that is their home. The hotel building is embellished with minarets and crescents. Decorating is simple, sophisticated, and charming. Big couches and modern pieces mix with antiques, a Norwegian wood stove, woven rugs hand-crafted locally, woven Welsh bedspreads, paintings of the district, and contemporary prints. Books, magazines, and fresh flowers abound.

Everyone books for the five-course set dinner. Patricia cooks in the country tradition, using locally reared meat and eggs from free-range hens. There is always homemade bread, and vegetarian meals can be provided. In an acre of walled garden, peaches, grapes, pears, cherries, and numerous varieties of apples are grown organically.

Literary buffs who don't drive can take a train from Paddington Station, London, to Ledbury, where a taxi will take them the two miles to the hotel. There they can wander over the 40 acres of wooded valley and park that Elizabeth Barrett Browning never forgot.

Proprietors: John and Patricia Hegarty. *Closed:* November 30 through February. *Recreational facilities:* Tennis, golf, and riding a short drive away. *Other facilities:* 2 lounges, garden. *Rooms:* 7 with bath. Suitable for wheelchair guests. Advance reservations are accepted for a 2-day minimum stay. 2-day reduction; winter breaks. Not suitable for children. Moderate. *Restaurant service:* Dinner (by reservation). *Credit cards:* Amex, Diners, Master, Visa. *How to get there:* Hope End is 2 miles north of Ledbury. Ask directions in the town. *Telephone:* (0531) 3613.

cester

Lifton, Devon

ARUNDELL ARMS

Oh, the gallant fisher's life!
It is the best of any;
'Tis full of pleasure, void of strife,
And 'tis beloved by many.

Izaak Walton, 1653

In the garden of this inn is one of the last two cockpits left in England. An octagonal stone and thatched building, it is now The Rod Room, and around the sawdust ring where the cocks once fought stands a rack for the fishermen's rods. The Arundell Arms is possibly England's premier fishing inn. If you ever thought you'd like to learn to fish, this is the place for you. Literally thousands of people have learned here in three- or four-day courses or with private lessons. An experienced fisherman can be accompanied by a ghillie, and both lessons and ghillie should be booked in advance. All gear, including waders, can be hired.

But the ivy-clad inn, in the middle of a tiny village, is not for fishermen only. One of us stayed here back in the 1930s and thought then that it was the epitome of what an old English inn should be. The rooms and furnishings have been considerably modernized since, losing some of the wonderful old atmosphere, but it is attractively done with big comfortable chairs before log fires — a friendly place with a dining room recommended in British food guides. One of its two bars is the village pub.

While the fishermen of the party are after salmon and trout, others can explore the mysterious Dartmoor, all 300 square miles of it. Lifton is right on the edge of this land of tors and ghostly mists, *Hound of the Baskervilles* country.

Proprietor: Anne Voss-Bark. *Closed:* A few days at Christmastime. *Recreational facilities:* Fishing for salmon, sea trout, and trout from the hotel; ocean swimming, surfing, deep-sea fishing, golf, riding, and hunting a short drive away. Snipe and pheasant shoots are run from the hotel from November to January. *Facilities for children:* Baby-listening. *Other facilities:* Lounge, cocktail bar, public bar, garden, game room with table tennis, darts, and skittle alley. *Rooms:* 28, 26 with bath, all with telephone, TV, and tea-making. 2 self-catering apartments for four people each, both with use of all hotel lounges and facilities. Suitable for wheelchair guests. 2-day reduction; 2-day breaks. Children under 16 free if sharing. Moderate. *Restaurant service:* Luncheon, snacks, dinner. *Credit cards:* Amex, Master, Visa. *How to get there:* Lifton is on Route A30 about 4 miles east of Launceston. *Telephone:* (0566) 84666. *Agent in the United States:* Best Western. [T]

WHITE HART

Hart, for thine Hospitality
Then be thine Horn exalted
Which Cornucopia flowed for me
Since at thy doors I halted.

G. K. Chesterton, 1933

Spectacular Lincoln Cathedral, on a hilltop, dominates this historic city and is an impressive sight, especially when it's illuminated at night. Sharing the hilltop is Lincoln Castle, founded by William the Conqueror in 1068, and in between the two stands the ancient White Hart. Among its famous visitors, besides Chesterton, have been Edward, Prince of Wales, who hosted a dinner party here in 1927 and signed the menu, and Prince Charles, who still drops in for dinner.

Today's lounge was the coaching yard in the days of the great coaching age. Now enclosed, it holds an original Chippendale breakfront filled with antique Rockingham china on which hotel meals were once served. A collection of silver candlesticks, used daily in times past, now must be shown behind glass. Bedrooms come in all shapes and with all styles of furniture, from fine antiques to modern built-ins.

Cobbled streets lined with medieval houses, many now antique shops, lead to the lower town. The Newport Arch, marking the north gate of the Roman town that was on this site, is one of only three Roman arches left in the world and is the only one traffic drives under. Lincoln is a city, and the White Hart is an atmospheric city hotel, though less personal than a small owner-run guest house. If you go, reserve ahead and ask for a room facing the cathedral.

Manager: Roger Brown. *Facilities for children:* Baby-listening. *Other facilities:* 2 lounges, TV lounge, cocktail bar, public bar, roof patio. *Rooms:* 52 with bath, 24-hour room service, TV, telephone and tea-making; 12 suites. Elevator. Weekend breaks. Moderate. *Restaurant service:* Luncheon, snacks, tea, dinner. *Credit cards:* Amex, Carte Blanche, Diners, Master, Visa. *Telephone:* (0522) 26222. *Agent in the United States:* THF. [T]

THE CONNAUGHT

> I have seen the greatest wonder which the world can show to the astonished spirit. I have seen it and am still astonished, . . . I mean London.
>
> *Heinrich Heine,* 1826

If luxury is sumptuous living in great ease and comfort, the dignified Connaught, which attracts guests from all over the world, is the place to find it. Guests are welcomed by a doorman in silk top hat and white gloves. Beds are turned down and towels are changed twice daily at this quiet hotel in the heart of Mayfair, near famous Berkeley Square, but the elegance is unostentatious. The public rooms have a patina of well-bred grace and charm.

At breakfast time in the mahogany-paneled dining room, the Victorian era is recaptured. Kippers, kedgeree, grilled kidneys, and finnan haddock are served on fine china embellished with the hotel's crest. Many gourmets say that the Connaught serves some of the best food in Britain. We try to have dinner there once every time we are in London. If you choose carefully from the extensive menu, your meal will be no more expensive than at most good restaurants.

It would be difficult to overpraise the quality of the Connaught. If you can afford it, it's well worth the splurge. But book months ahead of time: This hotel is almost always full.

Manager: Paolo Zago. *Special facilities:* 2 lounges, cocktail bar. *Rooms:* 89 with bath, TV, and telephone. Elevator. Very expensive. *Restaurant service:* Luncheon, tea, dinner. *Credit cards:* Master. *Mailing address:* Carlos Place, London W1. *Telephone:* (01) 499 7070.   [T]

DURRANTS HOTEL

> No one can tell where the West End will be next year. It is always moving to the country and never arriving there.
> *Augustus Hare,* 1878

In the West End, behind a Regency facade, there is a quintessentially British hotel that is much like a venerable gentlemens' club. Oak paneled walls, oil paintings, leather chairs, and dignified, hospitable service contribute to its restful atmosphere. Most of its comfortable bedrooms have simple modern furniture, with big puffs on the beds.

A friend wrote to us of it, "This is the kind of small London hotel people should look for — good atmosphere, reasonable price, and convenient location behind Selfridges." Durrants is owner-managed, unusual for a hotel of this size in London.

George Street is three blocks from, and parallel to, Oxford Street, near the Wallace collection of paintings, sculptures, and armor. Hyde Park is a short walk away.

Proprietor: Mr. R.C. Miller. *Facilities:* 2 lounges, cocktail bar. *Rooms:* 104, 80 with bath, all with telephone and TV. Elevator. Moderate. *Restaurant service:* Luncheon, tea, dinner. *Credit cards:* Amex, Diners, Master. *Mailing address:* 26 George Street, London W1H 6BJ. *Telephone:* (01) 935-8131.

EBURY COURT

> The lighted shops . . . the innumerable . . . coaches,
> waggons, playhouses; all the bustle and wickedness . . .
> the crowds . . . the print-shops, the old book-stalls . . .
> the coffee-houses, the pantomimes — London itself, a
> pantomime and a masquerade . . .
>
> *Charles Lamb,* 1801

"Never will we stay anywhere in London but at the Ebury Court," say some friends we recently suggested it to. If you are the sort who prefers to be treated as a house guest, not merely as a customer, if you enjoy being called by name by the staff and asked if you've had your afternoon tea, if you like little parlors with chintz-covered furniture where you may talk to the other guests, if you will take your chances on getting a room with a four-poster or, on the other hand, getting one that is plain or too small, then you will like the Ebury Court.

Ebury Street — the very name conjures up romantic images of liveried footmen, ladies in floaty chiffon and garden-party hats, and gentlemen's clubs. That sort of Edwardian splendor is in the past, but a faint aura remains. As you walk the neighborhood streets it isn't difficult to imagine Edward VII alighting from a carriage to visit the Duchess of Duke Street. You can stroll to the neighborhood pub for lunch. It is not difficult to get into a conversation at these pubs; everyone crowds around, sharing little tables wherever there is room.

English country folk who have come up to London for a visit are predominant guests at Ebury Court, which is made up of five joined terraced houses. Near Buckingham Palace and Victoria Station, it is an excellent location for those who would like to take day trips by train to Canterbury, Eastbourne, or Brighton, and it is a few minutes' walk from the Heathrow Airport bus.

You will be happiest with the Ebury Court if you draw a good bedroom, so reserve early and ask for one. Even if you book at the last minute and get one of the smallest rooms, you may feel lucky to get one at all in this convenient location in central London. Ebury Court is one of London's best-known small hotels and has a devoted following.

Proprietors: Romer and Diana Topham. *Special facilities:* TV and writing rooms. *Rooms:* 39, 13 with bath, all with telephone. Ground-floor rooms. Elevator. Moderate. *Restaurant service:* Luncheon, dinner. *Credit cards:* Master, Visa. *Mailing address:* 26 Ebury Street, London, SW1W 0LU. *Telephone:* (01) 730 8147.

11 CADOGAN GARDENS

> O . . . what shall I say of London? All the towns that ever I beheld in my born days are no more than Welsh barrows and crumlecks to this wonderful sitty! . . . such a power of people going hurry skurry! Such . . . noise and halli-balloo! So many strange sites to be seen! O gracious!
> *Tobias Smollett, 1771*

If you stay at 11 Cadogan Gardens, you will find it a retreat from all noise and "halliballoo." You'll think yourself visiting a wealthy family just before the turn of the century, although the staff will be friendlier than you might have found had Hudson been in charge.

The Victorian character of the place has been carefully preserved and enhanced with period furniture. In a charming drawing room, you may write a letter at an antique kneehole desk, order afternoon tea with scones and jam topped off with clotted cream, or sit on a tufted damask-covered sofa before a fire while you sip a pre-dinner drink. The hotel is not licensed, but a porter will quickly send out for a bottle and arrange for mixers and ice. He will bring pâté and toast or a sandwich at any time, give you a list of recommended restaurants with menus, provide you with maps, arrange theater tickets, and tell you what exhibitions are on.

If you put them outside your bedroom door, someone will polish your shoes; if you request it, someone else will wash your car. A chauffered Rolls-Royce is ready to drive you around London or out to the country — for a suitable fee, of course, although there is no charge to be driven within a half-mile radius in the four-door saloon car. That makes it pretty handy to reach Harrods on a pouring day, where it should be easy to while away an afternoon; or you might prefer the Victoria and Albert Museum nearby. In sunny weather, ask for the key to the private

garden, which is shared with neighbors, and have someone carry out a deck chair or chaise. Nothing is too much trouble.

And how marvelous it is to be able to order a light supper when hurrying to go to the theater — a casserole of lamb in red wine with fresh vegetables, for instance, for about $6 *including tax and service*! If you want a bit more, there is a choice of soups, the pâté (chicken liver or duck with orange), fresh fruit in season, and cheese and biscuits. Other main courses are coq au vin and a third choice that changes daily.

But you must find this unique hotel, and that isn't easy the first time. First you find Cadogan Gardens off Sloane Street. Cadogan Gardens isn't just a street, it goes around in a circle. Eventually you will see an imposing house with 11 over the door. That's it. No name — just the number 11. Ring the bell, settle into a Victorian bedroom (some have bathrooms with big, deep bathtubs, no shower) in one of four connected houses, and have a lovely quiet time. This hotel never raises its voice.

Managers: Mark Fresson and Alan Eyers. *Recreational facilities:* Tennis, squash, sauna, indoor pool, riding, boat rental in Hyde Park, and boat trips on the Thames, all a short walk away. *Other facilities:* 3

drawing rooms, sitting room, garden, laundry and valet service, chauffer-driven Rolls-Royce. *Rooms:* 60 rooms with bath and telephone, TV available; suites. Children sharing free. Expensive to very expensive. *Mailing address:* 11 Cadogan Gardens, Sloane Square, London SW3 2RJ. *How to get there:* Cadogan Gardens is off Sloane Street. *Telephone:* (01) 730 3426. [T]

GORING HOTEL

> Yesterday forenoon, I went out . . . and plunged headlong into London, and wandered about all day . . . only to lose myself for the sake of finding myself unexpectedly among things that I have always read and dreamed about.
>
> *Nathaniel Hawthorne, 1855*

Almost an extension of Buckingham Palace, the Goring set aside whole floors for visiting royalty and its entourage for the last three coronations. All accounts were rendered to the royal chamberlain. Its visitors' book is a priceless memento of the many world personalities who have slept under its Edwardian roof — Winston Churchill, Prince Pierre of Monaco (Rainier's father), the Grand Duchess Xenia of Russia, the Greek princesses Margarita and Sophia. Trygve Lie was a guest when he was appointed the first secretary-general of the United Nations. The hotel was taken over as part of American Military headquarters in World War I.

A hotel under family ownership for three generations, the Goring has accumulated a store of anecdotes about its guests. An amusing one tells of an American bishop who was asked how he made holy water. "Oh, I just boil the hell out of it" was his quick reply.

Today, George Goring, grandson of the man who built the hotel in 1910, still runs the Goring, the first hotel in the world to be equipped with a bathroom and central heating for every bedroom. Those bathrooms, luxuriously renovated, now have nothing Edwardian about them, and the bedrooms, too, have been modernized. But the marble floors of the spacious lobby, covered with Aubusson rugs, and the decorative plaster-work on the high ceilings of the dignified lounge maintain the aura of the early part of the century. Between the Palace Mews and Victoria Station, near Eaton Square, this is an *Upstairs, Downstairs* hotel for upstairs people.

Proprietor: George Goring. *Special facilities:* Drawing room, 2 lounges, cocktail bar. *Rooms:* 100 with bath, TV, and telephone; elevator. Suitable for wheelchair guests. Reduced weekend rates November through March. Very expensive. *Restaurant service:* Luncheon, snacks, tea, supper, dinner. *Credit cards:* Amex, Diners, Master, Visa. *Mailing address:* Beeston Place, Grosvenor Gardens, London, SW1W 0JW. *Telephone:* (01) 834 8211. *Agent in the United States*: Josephine Barr. [T]

NUMBER SIXTEEN

The happiness of London is not to be conceived but by those who have been in it.

James Boswell

Number Sixteen, with the atmosphere of a fine country inn, is surely the most attractive and most luxurious pension in London. Decorating is top drawer—beautiful chintzes, antiques, fine paintings. Flowers in casual arrangements ornament tables. Breakfast is brought to each bedroom, and each has comfortable seating and a little refrigerator.

This small hotel started in a white Victorian terrace house, number 16, on a pretty residential street in Kensington and later extended into numbers 14, 15 and 17. The row of houses is to be preserved for its architectural charm. A subway station is a few steps away, and it's an easy walk to Harrods, Sloane Square, Hyde Park Corner, and Chelsea. The combination of beauty, comfort, and personal attention here offers a different and delightful experience in London.

Proprietor: Michael Watson. *Special facilities:* Lounge, TV lounge, cocktail bar, garden. *Rooms:* 32 with bath, TV, and telephone. Elevator. No children under 10. Moderate to expensive. *Credit cards:* Amex, Diners, Master, Visa. *Mailing address:* 16 Sumner Place, London SW7 3EG. *Telephone:* (01) 589 5232. [T]

WILBRAHAM

> A country gentleman should bring his lady to visit London as soon as he can, that they may have agreeable topics for conversation when they are by themselves.
> *Samuel Johnson,* 1777

"The Wilbraham? The Wilbraham! My dear, however did you find the Wilbraham?" asked Gerald Stretton, astonished. I was telling the visiting Englishman where we had stayed on our last visit to London. "But shhhhh. Don't tell anyone, or you'll never get in again if the Americans find it!"

An appealing row of joined terrace houses in Belgravia, with tubs of blue hydrangeas and bright Paris awnings at the entrance, this is where the English stay when they come down from the country for a bit of shopping. The dignified but cozy paneled lounge was a gentleman's library. Graceful stairways ascend in surprising places, and bedrooms vary greatly. Ours was small, but our friends had one that was comfortably large, so it depends a bit on luck and a great deal on how early you reserve. We were happy to get one at all when we telephoned from Scotland a week ahead.

Don't miss nearby Harrods, and bring film to photograph the displays in its food halls. You'll probably see nothing like them anywhere else in the world.

There is no formal dining room at the hotel, but the extensive bar-lounge menu ranges from a sandwich or homemade soup with crusty French bread for under $2.00, or omelettes, crepes, and fish, to a steak or a mixed grill with vegetables for under $10.00 — a welcome find in this expensive part of London. It's a relaxing spot for lunch if you are shopping in the Sloane Street area.

Manager: D.Mullane. *Facilities for children:* Baby-sitting. *Other facilities:* Lounge, TV lounge, cocktail lounge. *Rooms:* 57, 34 with bath, all with telephone. Moderate to expensive. *Restaurant service:* Snacks and dinner, except Sunday. *Mailing address:* 1 Wilbraham Place, London SW1X. *How to get there:* Wilbraham Place is off Sloane Street near Sloane Square. *Telephone:* (01) 730 8296.

Long Melford, Suffolk

BULL HOTEL

> There cannot be a cleanlier, civiller inn than this is; which bears all the marks of old gentility, and of having been a manor house.
>
> *John Byng,* 1787

About five hundred years ago the house that is now the Bull Hotel was built by a wealthy wool merchant. By 1580, the sign of the Bull was outside and the establishment was dispensing ale and hospitality. John Byng, author of the quotation above, might have stopped there in 1787.

For more than a century the timbered frontage was hidden from view by a brick front, erected with the idea of giving the old place an up-to-date appearance in keeping with the newly built Georgian inns of the coaching era. In 1935, the 9-inch-thick brickwork was removed, revealing a magnificent example of oak half-timbering, perhaps the most romantic of all types of English architecture.

When we arrived, guests were lingering over tea before the huge hearth, some 12 feet wide, of Elizabethan brickwork, spanned by a massive oak mantel beam carved by a sixteenth-century craftsman. Room 30, with a velvet love seat before a tiled fireplace in an alcove, was our favorite. If the bedrooms are haunted by history, the bathrooms are not. They would suit even those who prefer new high-rise hotels to historic lodgings.

Lovers of venerable architecture will want to visit the nearby church with its beautiful old stained-glass windows, and everyone will want to browse in some of the antique shops in the town.

Manager: M. DiSora. *Recreational facilities:* Fishing, riding, squash, and golf a short drive away. *Facilities for children:* Baby-listening, children's menu. *Other facilities:* 2 lounges, public bar. *Rooms:* 27 with bath, TV, telephone, and tea-making. Ground-floor rooms. 2-day breaks; children under 16 free if sharing. Moderate. *Restaurant service:* Luncheon, snacks, tea, dinner. *Credit cards:* Amex, Carte Blanche, Diners, Master, Visa. *How to get there:* Long Melford is on Route A134 about 3 miles north of Sudbury, where guests can be met at the railway station, and about 12 miles south of Bury St Edmunds. *Telephone:* (0787) 78494. *Agent in the United States:* THF. [T]

Ludlow, Shropshire

FEATHERS

> This is one of the best towns for a gentell family of small
> fortune to retire to, I have ever seen for it is cheap, well
> built, and clean, surrounded by a charming country; and
> river; and affords a theatre, public walks, an assembly
> once a fortnight, and annual races.
>
> *John Byng, 1784*

That was Ludlow when intrepid traveler John Byng described it. He must
have stepped into Feathers, a famous and ancient hostelry even then. The
mists of time have clouded its construction date, but it stood there in
1521, and the massive entrance door with its 350 iron studs is the original.
Renowned throughout the world for antiquity and architectural interest,
the Feathers, with its magnificently ornate façade, was one of the first
licensed hotels in England.

Our bedroom was comfortable with a good bathroom, but it was furnished in an uninspired hotel-modern style. Some bedrooms have
antiques, including four-posters, but book well ahead for these. In the
attractive stone and timbered restaurant the waitresses wore old-style
dresses with white mob caps. The menu was extensive and the food good.
The Feathers has the atmosphere of a city hotel where guests do not meet
easily.

One of the most romantic places in Britain, Ludlow was once a walled
Norman town guarding the Welsh border. Walk the same streets trod by
John Milton, and visit the cemetery where A. E. Housman lies. Did the
poor little princes, later murdered in the Tower, play together when they
lived in Ludlow? Were they even then in fear for their lives? When the
religious Catherine of Aragon, first wife of Henry VIII, was here, did she
pray in the Church of Saint Laurence, where you can kneel today? This is
a historian's dream town.

Proprietor: Osmond Edwards. *Recreational facilities:* Riding, tennis,
and indoor pool a short drive away. *Facilities for children:* Baby-listening. *Other facilities:* Lounge, 2 public bars. *Rooms:* 35 with bath, TV,
and telephone. 2-day reduction; Christmas program. Moderate. *Restaurant service:* Luncheon, snacks, dinner. *Credit cards:* Amex, Master,
Visa. *How to get there:* Ludlow is on Route A49 between Hereford and
Shrewsbury. *Telephone:* (0584) 5261. *Agent in the United States:* Joseph-
ine Barr.   [T]

PARKHILL HOTEL

> One of the drollest things I have ever seen was a wild
> horse window-shopping for a hat on the main street of
> Lyndhurst . . . she was looking through the plate glass
> with an expression of such wearied disdain, such utter
> cynical disgust, that I was surprised the management did
> not rush out to protest.
> *Ruth McKenney,* 1950

The Parkhill Hotel stands in the New Forest, where landowners hold ancient grazing rights. Their horses roam freely across gorse-splashed moors and stroll with a proprietary air down the streets of busy towns. Cattle guards keep them off main highways. This quiet country house outside the town center was once a boarding school where a grandson of Queen Victoria's was a pupil and T. S. Eliot taught.

Carved pineapples decorate the building, built in 1770 by the man who introduced the pineapple to England. French doors open to the terrace from the Georgian lounge, where tea is set out every afternoon. Chintz covers on deep armchairs, old hunting prints on walls, potpourri in Chinese bowls—all convey an air so very nice, so truly English that the modernized cocktail lounge disappoints; but it is a comfortable and friendly place where, before dinner, you will meet the other guests, many of whom have lived in British colonial possessions—Kenya, Rhodesia, India, Malta—most of their lives and are now retired back home.

Good English cooking was served to us in a pleasant dining room overlooking a putting green shaded by 200-year-old trees. Vegetables are grown in the hotel's kitchen gardens and greenhouse. Our smiling waitress said, "Thank you, Madame," every time she removed a plate.

The New Forest is high on our recommended list of places to see in Britain. Where else do you see ponies wandering casually through the streets as unconcerned as the residents walking past them?

Proprietor: P. T. Ames. *Closed:* January. *Recreational facilities:* Outdoor pool and sauna at the hotel; riding and tennis a short drive away. *Other facilities:* Lounge, cocktail bar, garden. *Rooms:* 18 with bath, TV, and telephone. Ground-floor rooms. 2-day reduction. No children under 8. Moderate. *Restaurant service:* Luncheon, dinner. *Credit cards:* Amex, Master, Visa. *How to get there:* The hotel is on Route B3056 east of the center of Lyndhurst. *Telephone:* (042 128) 2944. [T]

Malmesbury, Wiltshire

OLD BELL

> And now once more I shape my way
> Through rain or shine, through thick or thin,
> Secure to meet at close of day,
> With kind reception at an inn.
>
> *William Shenstone,* 1737

Behind a wisteria-hung Cotswold stone front, the Old Bell continues the tradition of the monastic guest house it once was. Old oak and mahogany, antique brass lighting fixtures, open fires, plants, and fresh flowers decorate the Old Bell today. The restaurant in this village inn has a somewhat citified air: sometimes there is dancing. Beside the River Avon, a two-level garden bounded by stone walls invites one to sit on rustic furniture of natural wood.

The hotel is in the center of the most ancient town in England, chartered by King Alfred in A.D. 880. There is a street bar where local residents gather and play darts. Next door is a fine Norman abbey that is open to visitors. The Old Bell is a professionally managed inn in a convenient location.

Proprietor: Harry Spengler. *Closed:* December 25 through January 3. *Recreational facilities:* Riding nearby. *Facilities for children:* Baby-listening. *Other facilities:* Lounge, cocktail bar, public bar, garden. *Rooms:* 19, 15 with bath, all with TV, telephone, and tea-making. 2-day breaks. Inexpensive to moderate. *Restaurant service:* Luncheon, snacks, tea, dinner. *Credit cards:* Amex, Diners, Master, Visa. *How to get there:* The hotel is in Malmesbury's center. Guests can be met at the Kemble railway station. *Telephone:* (0662) 2344. [T]

CARWINION

> There was a salty tang in the air, a freshness that came
> from the open sea beyond the estuary, and as the ships
> entered the main channel of the river the sea-gulls rose
> in the air and followed them.
>
> *Daphne Du Maurier,* 1941

On the romantic Cornish coast near Frenchman's Creek, which inspired
Daphne Du Maurier's novel of the same name, travelers can get a real taste
of English country-house life at Carwinion. The large stone house, added
to over the centuries and standing in 20 acres of subtropical gardens, is the
ancestral home of Anthony Rogers. He and his wife, Fiona, opened it to
paying guests to preserve the estate for his children and future generations.
An additional 200 acres has been given to the National Trust.

The atmosphere is warm and comfortable, as is the house, which is filled
with color and well-loved antique furniture. Paintings, mirrors, and bibelots
cover walls, mantels, and tables. Oriental rugs are on the floors. Bedrooms
are homey rather than grand. In the dining room, shelves of books line one
wall, and portraits of ancestors look down from others.

Guests gather together in the drawing room for pre-dinner drinks and
dine at a large mahogany table set with Georgian silver, Victorian glass, and
early eighteenth-century china. Fiona and Anthony do all the cooking. They
combine the best of English and French cuisine, using vegetables from their
own garden, fresh-caught fish from the adjoining river and sea, and meat
from local farms.

A path leads from the house through the woods to a beach and bathhouse
on the Helford River. It's an easy walk to the village of Mawnan Smith,
and Land's End is a short drive away. Carwinion was the setting for the
movie *My Son,* from the novel of the same name by Howard Spring.

Proprietors: Anthony and Fiona Rogers. *Recreational facilities:* River
swimming, sailing, and fishing at the house; ocean swimming, boat trips,
and golf nearby. *Other facilities:* Drawing room, garden. *Rooms:* 3 with
bath, TV, and tea-making. Moderate. *How to get there:* Mawnan Smith
is 5 miles south of Falmouth. In the village, take the left fork at the Red
Lion Inn. 500 yards uphill on the right is a white gate marked Carwinion.
Telephone: (0326) 250258.

SPREAD EAGLE HOTEL

> The Spread Eagle of Midhurst, that oldest and most revered of all the prime inns of this world.
>
> *Hilaire Belloc*

At the famous Spread Eagle, comfort and history live together, for it was already an inn in 1430, and the "new" extension was built in 1650. In Elizabethan days the Spread Eagle was a center of much feasting and merriment for the queen and her lords. If she walked in today, she would recognize the timbered lounge. Except for more comfortable seating, it hasn't changed since Elizabeth, with her court, watched through its windows the archers and villagers in the market square roast an ox and be "merrie." She might sleep in the same four-poster but wouldn't know what to make of the strange comfort of its inner-spring mattress.

The old courtyard has been freed by time from the jostling of Oliver Cromwell's men and the stagecoaches of later days, but the cobblestones will still vibrate to the clatter of the huntsmen's horses and the cry of the hounds on every December 26, Boxing Day. If we were to spend Christmas in England, this hotel is one where we might try to make a reservation. We would find church services in the ancient Roman town; afternoon teas before log fires, with a background of Christmas music; candlelight dinners with blazing plum puddings; drinking of the stirrup cup as the hunter's horn announces the Boxing Day meet assembling in the courtyard.

Anya Seton made the Spread Eagle a setting for her historical novel *Green Darkness,* calling it "frightfully ancient, all half-timbering, dim passages and smuggler's hideaways." As at all such vintage inns, the bedrooms vary, and there are some here that are rather small and plain, so reserve early and request a good one.

Proprietors: Sandy and Anne Goodman. *Recreational facilities:* Golf, riding, tennis, and squash nearby. *Facilities for children:* Baby-sitting and -listening. *Other facilities:* Lounge, 2 public bars, garden. *Rooms:* 27, 23 with bath, all with TV and telephone. Winter breaks; 3- or 4-day Christmas program. Inexpensive to expensive. *Restaurant service:* Luncheon, snacks, tea, dinner. *Credit cards:* Amex, Diners, Master, Visa. *How to get there:* Midhurst is on Route A286 about 10 miles north of Chichester. *Telephone:* (073 081) 2211. *Agent in the United States:* Best Western.   [T]

Moreton-in-Marsh, Gloucestershire

MANOR HOUSE HOTEL

> The coffee room of the best class of English inns, carpeted and curtained, the dark, rich hue of the old mahogany, the ancient plate, the four-post bed, the sirloin or mutton joint, the tea, muffins, Cheshire and Stilton, the ale, the coal-fire and The Times, form an epitome of England: . . . the tea is fragrant with Cowper's memory, and suggestive of East India conquest.
>
> *Henry Tuckerman,* 1845

This entrancing inn of mellow golden stone, dating from 1540, is indeed of the "best class of English inns," and today, in its Old World lounges, fires still make for a cheery atmosphere in which to enjoy an afternoon tea or a nightcap. The original building features a priest's hiding hole, a secret passage, and the Moot Room, where in days gone by town merchants settled their disputes. Twisting corridors lead to antique-filled chambers — one reputed to be haunted. In the new wing, built of the same golden stone, are attractive modern bedrooms and baths. The large garden is a haven of tranquility, completely enclosed by high stone walls.

The hotel is on the High Street, which has a number of antique shops. Roman Legions marched here nearly two thousand years ago, as this was part of the old Roman Fosse Way, which cut across Britain in the far-off past. For those history buffs who love other eras but insist on today's comforts, this Cotswold hotel is the perfect place to stay.

Proprietor: Michael Fentum. *Recreational facilities:* Indoor pool and sauna at the hotel. *Other facilities:* Lounge, cocktail lounge, garden. *Rooms:* 40, 38 with bath, all with TV and telephone. Suitable for wheelchair guests. Winter breaks; Christmas program. Moderate. *Restaurant service:* Luncheon, snacks, tea, dinner. *Credit cards:* Amex, Diners. *How to get there:* Moreton-in-Marsh is on Route A44 between Chipping Norton and Broadway or take the train from Paddington Station, London, to Moreton-in-Marsh. *Telephone:* (0608) 50501. [T]

Mousehole, Cornwall

LOBSTER POT

The loveliest village in England.

Dylan Thomas, 1937

Mousehole (pronounced Mow' zl) is an active little fishing village filled with craft shops. For those who don't want to drive, the Lobster Pot is an especially good place from which to explore Cornwall's sandy beaches, romantic coves, and smugglers' villages. Many local buses leave the village every hour, and in season some of them connect at Penzance with the frequent trains that arrive daily from London.

On a perch overhanging one of Cornwall's most picturesque harbors, this sixteenth-century building has cozy, cretonne-filled public rooms and immaculate, bright bedrooms, some of them quite small. Lobster, crab, and Helford oysters are specialties in the dining room. If you can't stay, stop in for a crab sandwich and draught beer at noon. This friendly little hotel has an international reputation, so expect to meet guests from many countries. The building is scheduled as of historic architectural interest. Minimum advance reservations are for three nights, but you can often get in for one or two nights if you telephone not too far ahead. In March, and from late October until Christmas week, if you stay three days, you can stay another day free.

It was from the Lobster Pot, while honeymooning there in July 1937, that Dylan Thomas wrote to a friend that he had married Caitlin MacNamara at the Penzance Registry Office "with no money, no prospect of money, no attendant friends or relatives, and in complete happiness."

Proprietors: John and Susan Kelly. *Closed:* Early January to mid-March. *Recreational facilities:* Deep-sea fishing a short walk away; ocean swimming, tennis, squash, and riding a short drive away. *Other facilities:* 2 lounges, TV lounge, cocktail bar. *Rooms:* 23, 20 with bath, all with TV and tea-making. Off-season rates; 3-day reduction; discount for children sharing; Christmas program. Inexpensive to moderate. *Restaurant service:* Luncheon, snacks, tea, dinner. *How to get there:* Mousehole is on the Channel coast a few miles south of Penzance. One can take a train from London to Penzance and a bus from Penzance to Mousehole (3 miles). *Telephone:* (0736) 731251.

New Milton, Hampshire

CHEWTON GLEN

> The New Forest, my readers are perhaps aware, was first enclosed by William the Conqueror as a royal forest for his own amusement.
>
> *Frederick Marryat,* 1840

This Georgian building, with new wings, was the home of Captain Marryat, a nineteenth-century novelist, when he wrote *Children of the New Forest.* It is decorated in a serenely graceful manner. Lovely fabrics harmonize with Oriental carpets before glowing fires, and with thick wall-to-wall carpets wherever there are no Orientals, even in the bathrooms. Bouquets of flowers are fresh each day. White garden furniture sparkles under colorful umbrellas on the main terrace, while ground-floor bedrooms have individual patios where you may breakfast in the sun. Even the ladies' lounge has walls padded with chintz and hung with old prints. The bedrooms, where beds are turned down each evening, are named for Marryat's literary characters.

The hotel is a fine example of unpretentious elegance. The staff, quietly friendly and genuinely solicitous, seem to know each guest by name in amazingly short order. The food is nothing short of splendid. Roast ribs of Scotch beef and baron of lamb are carved from a silver trolley. Fresh fish is a specialty. Try beluga caviar, local smoked trout, Scotch salmon, lobster soup, Dover sole from the nearby sea. The selection from the cheese board is famous — don't miss the Stilton — as is the remarkable wine list. Coffee with petits fours is served in the lounge.

Chewton Glen is set in parkland between the famous Solent, where our first America's Cup race was won, and the historic New Forest, where ponies wander through village streets and gaze into shop windows. The New Forest is now carefully protected by the people whose ancestors so rightfully resented their sufferings when William, some nine hundred years ago, uprooted them from their forest dwellings to make for himself a royal hunting preserve.

Proprietor: Martin Skan. *Recreational facilities:* Outdoor pool, tennis, and putting green at the hotel; squash, riding, deep-sea fishing, and

sailing a short drive away. *Other facilities:* Drawing room, lounge, cocktail lounge, library, billiard room, garden, laundry service, chauffeur service. *Rooms:* 45 — and 7 suites — with bath, TV, and telephone. Suitable for wheelchair guests. Off-season rates; 2-day midweek breaks; 4-day Christmas and 3-day New Year's programs. No children under 7. Very Expensive. *Restaurant service:* Luncheon, dinner. *Credit cards:* All. *How to get there:* Driving south from Lyndhurst toward Bournemouth, ignore all signs into New Milton. Turn left at the road marked Walkford and Highcliffe. Drive 1 mile, passing through Walkford, then take the second left, marked Chewton Farm Road. The hotel entrance is on the right. Guests can be met at Heathrow or Gatwick airport, the boats at Southampton, or the New Milton railway station. *Telephone:* (04252) 5341. *Agents in the United States:* David Mitchell, Scott Calder.   [T]

PERCY ARMS

This deed was done at Otterbourne,
About the breaking of the day.
Earl Douglas was buried by the bracken bush
And the Percy led captive away.

Anonymous

The hotel's name commemorates Lord Percy and the famous border battle of Otterburn in 1388. Once a posting house from the bygone era of coaching, the Percy Arms today is a comfortable blend of Old World charm and New World comfort, set amid the scenic splendor of Northumberland's moors.

Deep, soft chairs before log fires mix well with old oak settles, a Welsh cupboard, and converted oil lamps. Some bedrooms have traditional painted furniture; some are modern, but these are decorated with soft traditional prints. A "taste of England" menu is added to the regular offerings in the dining room, and snacks are available after restaurant hours, handy for late arrivals or those who get hungry before bedtime. Tea in the garden is nice on a sunny day.

One friend told us her room was noisy with music from the bar underneath. When we took this up with the management, they explained that these are the last rooms to be given out, and the bar closes at eleven. So if you want to go to sleep early, make sure you don't get a room over the bar.

Proprietors: Carl and Jean Shirley. *Recreational facilities:* Riding and fishing a short drive away. *Other facilities:* 2 lounges, TV lounge, cocktail bar, public bar, garden. *Rooms:* 30 with bath, telephone, TV, and tea-making. Suitable for wheelchair guests. Off-season rates; 2-day breaks; Christmas program. Children under 10 free if sharing, discount if in separate room. Moderate. *Restaurant service:* Luncheon, snacks, tea, dinner. *Credit cards:* Amex, Diners, Master, Visa. *How to get there:* The hotel is on Route A696. *Telephone:* (0830) 20261. *Agent in the United States:* Consort Hotels. [T]

SHARROW BAY

> We took our way on foot towards Pooley Bridge. . . .
> Artists speak of the trees on the banks of Ullswater . . .
> as having a peculiar character of picturesque intricacy
> . . . which their rocky stations and the mountain winds
> have combined to give them.
>
> *William Wordsworth*

Some hotels are situated in glorious countryside with spectacular views, and others are beautifully furnished with antiques. Then there are those with a relaxed and cordial atmosphere, and others renowned for flawless food and service. Sharrow Bay is one of the rare hotels that combines all such qualities.

Interiors are a marvelous confusion of soft couches, curvy chairs, intriguing books, paintings and prints and framed mottoes, figurines, clocks, and wild English lamps. Sherry in each bedroom greets the guest, as do fresh flowers and luxury colognes. Each dish that Francis Coulson, the owner-chef, serves looks like a picture in *Gourmet* magazine, and he visits every table asking if all is satisfactory. Brian Sack, his partner, attends to each guest's desires with easy graciousness. This is a very personal luxury hotel, a member of the renowned Relais et Chateaux Hotels. Its guest register boasts many famous names, among them opera star Joan Sutherland, a personal friend for whom Francis Coulson named a special dessert, the Joan Sutherland Bavarois. J.B. Priestley and Norman Vincent Peale have stayed here not long ago.

Walk along the shores of Lake Ullswater, as Wordsworth did when he saw all those dancing daffodils, or drift dreamily in a rowboat pushed off from the hotel's stone jetty. Relax over a highball while watching the sun drop behind the mountains in a blaze of splendor — from the lakeside terrace in summer or through the great bay window of the drawing room in cooler weather.

Our first choice of rooms would be in Bank House. It has its own drawing room, a dining room where its guests have breakfast, and seven bedrooms, each with a bathroom and lake views that are a treat for the

Bank House

eye. This old farmhouse had been transformed with exquisite taste into luxury quarters incorporating an old stone fireplace from Warwick Castle with graceful furniture, soft chairs, and Oriental rugs. We first heard of Sharrow Bay from an American who stated flatly that it was the best hotel in Europe.

Proprietors: Francis Coulson and Brian Sack. *Closed:* Late November through early March. *Recreational facilities:* Lake swimming at the hotel; boat rides a short walk away; golf and riding a short drive away. *Other facilities:* 2 lounges, garden. *Rooms:* 30, 26 with bath. Suitable for wheelchair guests. Minimum 2-day advance reservation. No children under 13. Expensive to very expensive. *Restaurant service:* Luncheon, tea, dinner. *How to get there:* From Route M6 take exit 40 to Route A66, then take Route A592 to Pooley Bridge. At the church take the lane signposted "Howton" and drive 2 miles farther. The hotel will arrange for a taxi from Penrith. *Telephone:* (08536) 301. *Agent in the United States:* David Mitchell.　　　　　　　　　　　　　　　　　　　　　　　　　　[T]

REEDS

> Our England is a garden
> And such gardens are not made
> By singing "Oh how beautiful!" and
> Sitting in the shade.
>
> *Rudyard Kipling,* 1911

The reason Reeds is open only four days a week, from Friday afternoon until Tuesday morning, is that Margaret Jackson devotes midweek to caring for four acres of garden. She raises vegetables and herbs used in the kitchen and flowers that adorn the rooms.

A delightful widow, Margaret thoroughly enjoys meeting people and welcomes them warmly to her lovely country house a mile from the sea on the north Cornwall coast. Her dinners are a treat, as she is a wonderful cook. Reeds is featured in the British *Good Food Guide.* Dining-room tables are laid with crisp linen, silver, and candles. Pre-dinner drinks are served in the hall lounge in front of a log fire. Everything is homemade—rolls, pastries, ice cream. Fresh local fish and meat are accompanied by the garden produce. Menus change daily and guests' favorites are prepared on request. A small wine list is well-chosen. Coffee can be enjoyed either at the table or in the study, again before a fire except when it's warm. Then it might be taken on the terrace.

Three large, attractive bedrooms, some with views over treetops to the ocean, each have twin beds, two comfortable armchairs, and modern bathrooms. Staying at Reeds is so much like visiting a friend that you'll probably want to send a thank-you note when you get home.

Proprietor: Margaret Jackson. *Closed:* Christmas. *Recreational facilities:* Ocean swimming and riding nearby. *Other facilities:* Lounge, TV room, garden. *Rooms:* 3 with bath and tea-making. Not suitable for children. Inexpensive. *How to get there:* From Route A39 just north of Bude, follow signs to Poughill (pronounced Pof-fil). Do not go into Bude. *Telephone:* (0288) 2841.

PEACOCK HOTEL

The river that runs by the old Hall's walls
Murmured to them as it murmers now;
The golden glow of the sunset falls
As it fell for them, on glade river, and bough.

Anonymous

A National Monument, the Peacock was built as a luxurious private home in 1652. Later it became the Dower House of Haddon Hall, possibly the finest stately home open to the public in England today. Haddon Hall was the ancestral home of the dukes of Rutland, whose coat-of-arms contains a peacock. Izaak Walton was a guest at the hotel and

fished in the River Derwent bordering the gardens, which received a Horticultural Society award for their beauty. Today your bedroom in this antique-lover's paradise may have a high-backed bed and Gothic windows with diamond-leaded panes, but it will also have thick wall-to-wall carpets. A plaque explains the five-foot peacock perched near the entrance:

> This peacock, which is considered to be the most skillful example of ceramic art ever to be made in England, was manufactured by MINTON's LTD. about 1850/51. The modelling was carried out by the celebrated artist and sculptor of Limoges, Paul Comolera, who was employed by Minton's for a period of three years. During this time only about five of these peacocks were in fact produced. The decoration is carried out in the majolica style, being hand-painted in soft coloured glazes.

The history of this peacock is even more interesting. It was sent to Australia to be exhibited in 1878, but a shipwreck sent it to the bottom off Victoria. Some years later, when a Mr. Miller salvaged the wreck, a cask was opened to reveal the peacock in perfect condition, not a chip in it. It remained in the Miller family until 1937. We didn't learn how it came to the Peacock, but this outstanding hotel could have no more appropriate symbol.

Manager: G. M. Gillson. *Recreational facilities:* Riding a short drive away. *Facilities for children:* Baby-listening. *Other facilities:* Lounge, cocktail bar, garden. *Rooms:* 20, 15 with bath, all with TV and telephone. 3-day reduction; 2-day breaks; Christmas program; reduction for children. Moderate. *Restaurant service:* Luncheon, snacks, tea, dinner. *Credit cards:* All. *How to get there:* The hotel is on Route A6 between Bakewell and Matlock, north of the junction with B6012. *Telephone:* (0629) 733518.

Rye, East Sussex

MERMAID INN

> The little old, cobble-stoned, grass grown, red-roofed town.
>
> *Henry James*

No one dared to interfere with the infamous Hawkshurst gang of smugglers who once caroused in this most renowned of the old smugglers'

inns. Rebuilt in 1420, the Mermaid has pla_____
its long history, and was already very old whe_____
1573. The Elizabethan Chamber, with a tremen_____
memorates her visit. Our bedroom was two stories _____
rafter across it at normal room height. A bewilderment _____
this way and that, reeking of antiquity and inviting explo_____
fancy may hear a faint rustle—a stealthy creak of the old sta____
presence not of today.

The dining room, beautiful with linen-fold paneling, is highly laude____
In the friendly tavern a giant fireplace stretches across one wall, a massive
time-blackened timber spanning the opening. Cooking paraphernalia of
past centuries ornaments the great hearth, where a priest's hiding hole is
cleverly concealed. Ancient swords hang on the walls.

The steep hills of Rye must be negotiated through some of the nar-
rowest and crookedest streets in England. Rye is so crowded with tourists
in season that it is a wonder that the medieval charm persists, but persist
it does. Henry James lived here for the last twenty years of his life. He
was visited at his home, Lamb House, by many literary greats, among
them Joseph Conrad, G. K. Chesterton, H. G. Wells, Rudyard Kipling,
Max Beerbohm, and frequently by his close friend Edith Wharton.
Surely most of them knew the Mermaid. After James's death, Lamb
House became the home of E. F. Benson, mayor of Rye and author of the
popular *Lucia* books, which have many scenes set in the town. Rumer
Godden also once lived at Lamb House.

Proprietor: M. K. Gregory. *Special facilities:* Lounge, cocktail bar.
Rooms: 27 with bath. 2-day reduction; 2-day breaks; 4-day Christmas
program. Moderate. *Restaurant service:* Luncheon, snacks, dinner.
Credit cards: Amex, Diners, Visa. *How to get there:* Rye can be reached
by train from London. The inn is on Mermaid Street. *Telephone:* (0797)
223065.   [T]

> Cornwall that I know
> ...nd, because it smells
> ...y breath of heather-bells
> ...salt.
>
> *Arthur Symons*

...ior is warm and welcoming, due to the
...guests like old friends. They are refugees
from ... have filled their country house with fresh
flowers, good an... ...nolstery fabrics, Wedgwood china, enam-
eled clocks, and paintings o. ...al scenes, some of which are for sale. We
liked the stripped pine furniture in the rather smallish bedrooms.

Mary is the chef and her food is recommended by Michelin. The wine
list is strong on French wines. Andrew cooks breakfast for everyone. It's
lovely to have it in the conservatory when weather permits, or even outdoors
when it's really warm. A swimming pool is bordered by palm trees and has
a sheltered terrace so guests can sit in or out of the sun. About a five-minute
walk away through the woods is another building on the property called
Wheal Eliza. It has been divided into two parts, one a home for the assistant
manager. The other half, with its own front door, has been converted to
two bedrooms with baths and a dining-sitting room where breakfast is
served. The drive around to it by road takes about five minutes.

Those traveling in cold weather will find Boscundle Manor a particularly
good spot, with its double-glazed windows and new central heating system
and insulation. Wood fires give an added glow, even on the darkest days.

Proprietors: Andrew and Mary Flint. *Closed:* December 23rd to mid-
February. *Recreational facilities:* Outdoor pool and Jacuzzi at the house;
riding and ocean swimming nearby. *Other facilities:* Living room, conservatory, cocktail bar, laundry facilities, and garden. *Rooms:* 9 with bath,
telephone, and TV. Moderate. *Restaurant service:* Luncheon and dinner
by reservation available daily (for house guests only on Sundays and
holidays). *Credit cards:* Amex, Master, Visa. *How to get there:* 2 miles east
of Saint Austell on Route A390, turn left at a small signpost for Tregrehan,
almost opposite the Saint Austell Garden Centre. Find Boscundle Manor
about 100 yards on the left. *Telephone:* (072681) 3557.

TREGOOSE OLD MILL

> Welcome ever smiles
> And farewell goes out sighing.
>
> *William Shakespeare*

This fifteenth-century mill house is one of the hidden delights of England. Sue Cameron's work in TV production and movies, and as a professional photographer, took her all over the world. After nineteen years, she wanted a change and bought a converted mill and eight acres beside a stream. She has hens, geese, goats, donkeys, dogs, an apple orchard, and a hive of bees to make honey.

If you are lucky enough to get one of the four bedrooms, you'll eat supremely well, discussing your dinner choice with Sue in the morning or when you telephone. There are three choices for each course every day, but she will cook something special should you desire. That might be salmon or local trout baked in herbs and wine, sole Veronique, steak Diane or steak au poivre, veal Leone, roast duck for two with black cherry sauce, roast pheasant, or perhaps young chicken filled with your choice of stuffing. If you borrow gear and catch a trout, Sue will cook it for you. Although the wine selection is large, if you would like a particular wine and let her know in advance, she will make sure you have it with your dinner.

The dining room has books lining one wall and a single long table, candlelit at dinner time. It's in what was the miller's living quarters. You'll probably take coffee and liqueurs before a fire in the spacious lounge, the original mill, where we sat under what are probably the largest beams we've ever seen. Breakfast is whenever you care to get up. Sue says, ''I fit in with my guests. They do not fit in with me.''

Proprietor: Sue Cameron. *Recreational facilities:* Trout fishing at the house; ocean swimming, deep-sea fishing, and riding nearby. *Other facilities:* Sitting room, lounge, garden. *Rooms:* 4, 1 with bath. Inexpensive. *Restaurant service:* Dinner by reservation. *How to get there:* Do not go into Saint Columb Major. From Route A3059 to Newquay, turn left opposite the sign for Saint Columb Major. Take this road, keeping left, for 1 1/2 miles. Tregoose Old Mill is the last house before the road crosses the river. *Telephone:* (0637) 880559.

GREENWAY

> Such an old house fills an American with an indefinable
> feeling of respect . . . its central English sturdiness, its
> oaken vertebrations so humanized with ages of use and
> touches of beneficent affection.
>
> *Henry James,* 1875

If prizes were given for hotels that most resembled the private manor of a person of wealth, Greenway would be one of the winners. Built in 1584, it was just such a place until this century. As we sat in deep chairs of country chintz and sofas covered with velvet, before blazing fires in baroque fireplaces, we felt a pleasure that comes of being a part of a vanished era.

Third-floor bedrooms have beams and alcoves, while one on the second floor was a half-tester bed. The lounge and cocktail bar look onto formal gardens, topiary, and 37 acres of parkland. Lunch can be taken by the lily pond in the summer. Guests should make dinner reservations (jacket required) when reserving their rooms. This owner-managed hotel will arrange for you to rent golf clubs or fishing equipment. No one could help but like Greenway; it has quality.

Proprietors: Tony and Maryan Elliott. *Recreational facilities:* Riding, golf, and dry-fly trout fishing a short drive away. *Other facilities:* Drawing room, lounge, cocktail bar, garden. *Rooms:* 11 with bath, TV, and telephone. Winter and weekend breaks. No children under 7. Expensive to very expensive. *Restaurant service:* Luncheon Sunday through Friday, dinner. *Credit cards:* Amex, Carte Blanche, Diners, Master, Visa. *How to get there:* The hotel is on Route A46, 3 miles south of Cheltenham. *Telephone:* (0242) 862 352. *Agent in the United States:* Abercrombie and Kent. [T]

PARROCK HEAD FARM

> . . . a genial hearth, a hospitable board, and a refined
> rusticity.
> *William Wordsworth*

Before a hearty fire we sat enjoying drinks and good conversation with
other guests in a spacious lounge. It was on the second floor of an extension added to the original 1677 farmhouse. Through floor-length windows we watched a little sheep dog herd his charges a few fields away.
The white sheep all seemed to be wearing black and white striped socks,
the markings on their legs being peculiar to the particular breed. Nearer
the house, farm lads drove calves into a barn. The scene was bucolic, but
the inn was sophisticated, a rare combination.

Patricia Holt's sense of style is apparent in the blend of antique and
modern furnishings. The extension was once a barn, and under its high
beams, rough white plaster walls are the background for antique oak
pieces, bulky brown couches, chairs in rust linen, an enormous straw
basket for logs, a table set up for games, a gleaming copper coal hod. The
fireplace wall is all stone. Next door, a low-beamed library is lined with
books, and a large table is spread with magazines and pamphlets describ-
ing local attractions. A new building just steps away holds most of the
bedrooms, which have pale pine furniture and flowered Continental
quilts with matching draperies. Two bedrooms are labeled family rooms
for three people, but they really are a double and a single room sharing
one bath, a good setup for a couple traveling with a third party.

Dinner is à la carte. This is one of the few small inns in which we could
enjoy traditional roast beef with Yorkshire pudding and roast potatoes.
Except in large hotels, this is usually served only at Sunday noon, when
we are looking for just a light snack. A strawberry and apple pie finished
a satisfying meal.

Mr. Holt is a barrister, but Parrock Head is a working farm with Mrs.
Holt's son in charge. This is one of the best values in Britain. Unless you
are very lucky, you must book well in advance.

Proprietor: Patricia Holt. *Closed:* December and January. *Special
facilities:* Lounge, library, cocktail bar, garden. *Rooms:* 10 with bath,
TV, and tea-making. Ground-floor rooms. Reduction for children sharing. Inexpensive. *Restaurant service:* Dinner. *How to get there:* The farm
is in Woodhouse Lane west of the village of Slaidburn. Ask directions in
the village. *Telephone:* (020 06) 614.

THE OXENHAM ARMS

> The stateliest and most ancient abode in the hamlet.
> *Eden Phillpotts,* 1899

If you are a lover of ancient inns and turn all funny at the sight of worn flagstones, sloping floors, medieval beams, and walk-in fireplaces, The Oxenham Arms is your kind of place.

Writers such as Eden Phillpotts and Charles Kingsley have described it in their novels. First licensed in 1477, the inn is believed to have been built by monks in the twelfth century. After the dissolution of the monasteries, it became a dower house of the Burgoyne family, and it's now listed as an Ancient Monument.

Chairs of leather, velvet, and cretonne are drawn up around a huge stone fireplace in the cozy main living room. A granite pillar supports a great beam in the busy dining room. An interesting room is a small lounge where a monolith is set into a wall. The theory of archaeologists is that the monastic builders placed their house around this prehistoric stone shaped by man 5,000 years ago. Notwithstanding deep digging, its foundations have never been reached.

Smallish to average-sized, low-beamed bedrooms—numbers 4 and 9 are the larger—are reached by worn stone steps, up a few here, down a few there. Diamond-paned windows and fresh flowers lend more charm. Two bedrooms, each with private bath and having the exclusive use of a sitting room, are in a cottage directly across the street.

Surprisingly, the owner is an American, but his wife is British. The Oxenham Arms is in a village on the edge of Dartmoor. The colorful Mid-Devon Foxhounds meet in its forecourt. It's unlikely a history buff could resist the lure of this place.

Proprietor: James Henry. *Recreational facilities:* Riding and windsurfing nearby. *Other facilities:* Lounge, TV room, public bar, garden. *Rooms:* 10, 6 with bath, all with TV and tea-making. 3-day reduction. Inexpensive to moderate. *Restaurant service:* Luncheon, snacks, dinner. *Credit cards:* Amex, Diners, Master, Visa. *How to get there:* South Zeal is signposted on Route A30 just east of Okehampton. *Telephone:* (0837) 840244.

GEORGE OF STAMFORD

> Great rambling, old places they are, with galleries and
> passages and staircases, wide enough and antiquated
> enough to furnish materials for a hundred ghost stories,
> supposing we should ever be reduced to the lamentable
> necessity of inventing any.
>
> *Charles Dickens*

Although many old inns proudly boast a sinister past, this ancient
Dickensian inn has always retained a grave respectability. King Charles I
stayed twice in 1645, and centuries later Sir Walter Scott found it a favorite resting place between London and Scotland.

It is probable that a part of the George was standing here in the
middle of the tenth century. Thick exterior walls of what were two reli-

gious houses that bounded the old inn are now deep inside the present handsome building. These were "hospitals," one for pilgrims and knights on their way to Jerusalem, the other a charity "hospital" that gave free food and lodging to poor travelers. The word "hospital" at that time meant simply a place giving hospitality. Visitors will see on their left as they enter a door marked "London" and on their right a door marked "York." These two old paneled rooms were the waiting rooms in which passengers assembled while waiting for their coaches to change horses in the inn yard.

Under the same beams where those in centuries past have gathered before the inn's great hearths, today's guests will enjoy deep, comfortable chairs and fine antiques. They can stroll on graveled walks and sit under an ancient mulberry tree in the beautifully landscaped Monastery Garden. Early-morning tea and a newspaper are brought to each bedroom. The paneled dining room of the George was one of only three outside London that the writer E. V. Lucas thought worth going to, and its renown continues. Make a dinner reservation when you book your room. Stop in for midmorning coffee or afternoon tea; drinks and snacks can be had all day. Although less personal than a small owner-operated inn, this very superior hotel will give a real glimpse into the English past and should delight any traveler.

Manager: Jolyon Gough. *Recreational facilities:* Outdoor pool, sauna, and boat rental a short walk away. *Facilities for children:* Babysitting and -listening. *Other facilities:* 2 lounges, cocktail bar, public bar, garden, gift shop. *Rooms:* 35 with bath, TV, and telephone; suites. Weekend breaks; reduction for children sharing. Moderate. *Restaurant service:* Luncheon, early and late snacks, tea, dinner. *Credit cards:* Amex, Diners, Master, Visa. *How to get there:* Stamford is just off the main Route A1 between London and Edinburgh, a few miles south of Grantham. The hotel will pick up passengers at trains in Stamford or Peterborough or at Heathrow Airport. *Telephone:* (0780) 55171.

Stratford-upon-Avon, Warwickshire

SHAKESPEARE

> Let Beauty with the sun arise
> To Shakespeare tribute pay.

> *Anonymous*

Imagine yourself sleeping in a bedroom called Midsummer Night's Dream, or in one named Twelfth Night, Much Ado About Nothing, or Love's Labour's Lost. The naming of the rooms after Shakespeare's plays was started by David Garrick, the revered actor, when he was a guest in the hotel in 1769. You can dine in As You Like It and have a drink in the cozy Measure for Measure pub.

With its nine timbered gables, this beautiful Tudor building, once an enormous private home, is the largest of the very old buildings in this historic town. The boy Shakespeare passed it daily on his way to school. He must have mingled in the throngs at the weekly market, still held just up the street, where we bought a blue and white china sugar bowl that reminds us daily of Stratford.

The low-beamed rooms, with vast, open fireplaces, are full of charm and character. The bedrooms are rather small for a first-class hotel, and some are completely modern; but in Stratford you won't be spending much time in your room. About 1912 a guest wrote that "it is almost a sufficient curiosity in itself to repay one for the trip."

Manager: Tim Ireson. *Recreational facilities:* Tennis, squash, sauna, and an indoor pool a short walk away; riding and golf a short drive away. *Facilities for children:* Baby-sitting and -listening. *Other facilities:* 2 lounges, cocktail bar, public bar. *Rooms:* 66 with bath, TV, telephone, and tea-making. 2-day breaks; 50% discount for children under 14 sharing (free if under 5). Expensive. *Restaurant service:* Luncheon, early and late snacks, tea, dinner. *Credit cards:* Amex, Diners, Master, Visa. *How to get there:* The hotel is on Chapel Street. From London, you can take a train from Paddington Station or a bus from Victoria Station. *Telephone:* (0789) 294771. *Agent in the United States:* THF.   [T]

STRATFORD HOUSE

Yes, he,
The pride of England
Glistened like a star,
And beckoned us to Stratford.

Robert Leighton

The walled entrance courtyard filled with flowering plants caught our eye as we walked along Sheep Street. Its charm beckoned us inside to find this small Georgian house, completely refurbished just a few years ago by Peter and Pamela Wade. Their own furniture, china, and pictures fill the interior of what is now a gem of a bed and breakfast lodging, right in the center of eveything you'll want to see in Stratford.

The bar is in a corner of the living room and run on the honor system —make your own drink and jot down what you take. Breakfast is exceptional, and Peter makes the marmalade himself. The Wades assist their guests in every way possible. They enjoy helping them plan tours of the area and will make every effort to obtain theater tickets, although they advise advance booking. They make recommendations among the many restaurants and pubs that abound on the surrounding streets. Peter operates a private-car tour service. He will drive guests on day tours from Stratford-on-Avon, returning to Stratford House each night. This charming small hotel is a real find and certainly our first choice in Stratford-upon-Avon.

Proprietors: Peter and Pamela Wade. *Closed:* Christmas week. *Recreational facilities:* Indoor pool, boat rental and boat trips on the Avon, tennis, and squash a short walk away; riding and hunting a short drive away. *Other facilities:* Lounge. *Rooms:* 10, 8 with bath, all with TV and tea-making. Suitable for wheelchair guests. Off-season rates. Discount for children under 9 sharing. Not suitable for infants. Moderate. *Credit cards:* Amex, Diners, Master, Visa. *How to get there:* The hotel is on Sheep Street, close to the Royal Shakespeare Theatre. From London, take a train from Paddington Station or a bus from Victoria Station. From the Heathrow or Gatwick airport take a special Flightlink bus to Warwick. Guests can be met anywhere in Britain — at any airport, in central London, or at any other place — if prior arrangements are made. *Telephone:* (0789) 68288. [T]

PLUMBER MANOR

> The beautiful Vale of Blakemore or Blackmoor...an
> engirdled and secluded region for the most part untrodden
> yet by tourist or landscape painter....
>
> *Thomas Hardy,* 1891

When he wrote *The Return of the Native,* Hardy lived in Sturminster Newton
with his wife, Emma, who called that "our happiest time." In the midst
of his "beautiful Vale of Blakemore or Blackmoor," Plumber Manor has
been in the same family since the seventeenth century. To maintain their
inherited 400-acre estate, the Prideaux-Brune family turned their Jacobean
home into a country-house hotel.

Their friendliness and hospitality gives this lovely house a special warmth
and character. Antiques from the family collection are found throughout,
and the main staircase is lined with portraits of family members who have
lived here over the centuries. Half the bedrooms are in the main house, all
elegantly furnished and with spacious bathrooms. A stone coach house close
by, reached by a garden path, was converted to six large modern bedrooms
with fine furniture and pretty floral fabrics.

Brian Prideaux-Brune already had a flair for cooking when the hotel
opened, and his talents have long since been recognized by all major food
guides. Brother Tim presides behind the bar; Richard and Alison give personal attention to detail and service. This appealing manor is now a luxurious hotel that successfully blends all modern comforts into its ancient
heritage.

Proprietor: Richard Prideaux-Brune. *Closed:* February and the first two
weeks of November. *Recreational facilities:* Golf, riding, and clay-pigeon
shooting nearby. *Other facilities:* Lounge, sitting room, cocktail lounge,
garden. *Rooms:* 12 with bath, telephone, TV, and tea-making. Ground-floor
rooms. 2-day minimum advance reservation for weekends; 2-day reduction
midweek; off-season rates. No children under 12. Moderate to expensive.
Restaurant service: Dinner by reservation (closed to the public on Monday).
How to get there: From A357, slighty southwest of Sturminster Newton,
take Hazelbury Bryan Road. Go over a mile and find Plumber Manor on
the left. *Telephone:* (0258) 72307. *Agent in the United States:* Abercrombie
and Kent.   [T]

CLOSE

> Every step you take in such a house confronts you in one way or another with the remote past. You feast upon the pictorial, or inhale the historic.
>
> *Henry James,* 1877

Built in 1596 as the home of a wealthy Cotswold wool merchant, the Close has a richly deserved reputation for beauty and comfort. Its lounge was originally the central courtyard, enclosed in Georgian times with a superb domed ceiling and oval window overhead. The highly lauded dining room provides an elegant background with sparkling silver and candlelight. Monsieur Jean-Marie Lauzier, the host, is a confrere of the Chevaliers du Tastevin, which certainly ensures the quality of the wine cellar. Rooms with shell-shaped niches that hold fresh flower arrangements have Adam ceilings and display fine paintings. Bedrooms have names like Rose, Tower, and Dove, and even the beamed ones on the third floor are spacious.

While having a proper afternoon tea in the serene and sunny walled garden, it is hard to realize that the front door of the Close opens onto a main street of this prosperous old town with its Elizabethan market hall. A wealth of antique shops in which to find treasure makes this a good spot for those who can spend only a few days out of London.

Even winter has its attractions, especially the spectacle of a meet of the hunt in the market square or a day at a local point-to-point. More active visitors might want to engage a horse to ride over the unspoiled countryside and then return to sit before the warmth of a friendly log fire. The Close is a fine selection for the discriminating traveler.

Proprietor: Jean-Marie Lauzier. *Recreational facilities:* Tennis and riding a short drive away. *Facilities for children:* Baby-sitting and -listening. *Other facilities:* Lounge, cocktail bar, garden. *Rooms:* 12 with bath, TV, telephone, and tea-making. 2-day reduction for children under 14 sharing (free if under 3). Moderate to expensive. *Restaurant service:* Luncheon, snacks, tea, dinner. *Credit cards:* Amex, Carte Blanche, Diners, Master, Visa. *How to get there:* The hotel, at 8 Long Street, will arrange to have a taxi meet the train at Kemble. *Telephone:* (0666) 52272. *Agent in the United States:* Ray Morrow. [T]

THORNBURY CASTLE

> Here moved on,
> In stately minuet lords, with doublets slashed
> And ladies rustling in the stiff brocade.
> *Lydia Sigourney,* 1856

Thornbury Castle's turbulent history reaches back to the tenth century, before it was seized by William the Conquerer. In 1510 the Duke of Buckingham received a license from Henry VIII to fortify and crenelate the castle. Ten years later the Duke was executed at Tower Hill after having been indiscreet enough to make some rude remarks about Henry that were heard by Cardinal Wolsey and reported to the King. Henry appropriated the castle and stayed there with Ann Boleyn. Mary Tudor lived in it for some years. She returned it to the descendants of the Duke of Buckingham after she became Queen.

In 1966 the castle was acquired by Kenneth Bell who established it as a renowned restaurant, winning many awards. Luncheon is a three-course meal with six or seven choices per course. (Prepare to pay top price.) Dinner is à la carte. Among the first courses, you might choose Coquilles St. Jacques, mousse of Cornish crab, or cream of watercress soup. Continue, perhaps, with Severn salmon baked in pastry, paupiette of veal with apricot and sorrel stuffing, or venison pie. Desserts include Thornbury treacle tart, honey and almond ice cream, strawberries on a meringue with Grand Marnier, and always a fine selection of farmhouse cheeses. Two dining rooms are baronial, with paneled walls, heraldic shields, and great open fires. There may be a cover charge for the dining room in which a pianist plays, so ask about that.

A drawback to many country-house hotels with busy restaurants open to the public is that their lounges become uncomfortably crowded by diners waiting to be seated. Not so at Thornbury Castle, which has one lounge for residents and another for restaurant patrons. Furnishings in both are sumptuous.

Bedrooms are opulent, with lofty ceilings, deep-piled carpets, and upholstered couches and chairs. Some have tall oriel windows and four-poster beds expensively draped with beautiful fabrics. There's a great feeling of romance to sleeping in rooms slept in by the most famous monarchs of England. They may have had absolute power over their subjects, but you'll enjoy luxury and comforts they never knew.

The castle is surrounded by its own vineyard, and you can join in the harvest when the grapes are ripe. Thornbury Riesling Sylvaner is included on the extensive wine list. Thornbury Castle is for the traveler who wants sybaritic perfection and is willing to pay for it.

Proprietor: Kenneth Bell. *Closed:* Christmas week. *Facilities:* 2 lounges, garden. *Rooms:* 12 with bath, telephone, and TV. 1 ground-floor room. No children under 12. Expensive to very expensive. *Restaurant service:* Luncheon, dinner. *Credit cards:* All. *How to get there:* From Route M4, take Route A38 to Route B4061. In Thornbury, drive downhill to the end of High Street, take the left fork, and see the gate lodge entrance to the castle by the prominent tower of the parish church. *Telephone:* (0454) 412647. *Agent in the United States:* Scott Calder. [T]

Upper Slaughter, Gloucestershire

LORDS OF THE MANOR

> Upper Slaughter . . . hidden in the complex and sinuous folds of the hills . . . is a village after the pattern of Hans Anderson.
>
> *J. J. Massingham,* 1932

Lords of the Manor stands in a quaint village. The ivy-clad manor was the home of the Witts family for more than two hundred years until it was converted to a hotel in 1972 by Francis Witts, a London banker. It is managed by his cousin and her husband, Gabrielle and Anthony de Trafford.

In a traditional drawing room there is English chintz on soft furniture, a log fire, and a wall of tall windows that overlook garden and meadow. Bamboo furniture covered in summery green, blue, and white decorates a garden room. Some bedrooms have antique furnishings, one, a splendid four-poster; others, in newly converted attached buildings, are pretty and inviting but more modern. Portraits of Witts ancestors decorate walls. On a menu that changes daily and is recommended in food guides, there is a good choice of main dishes — salmon, trout, duck, pheasant — and homemade soups, pâtés, and desserts. Bar snacks at noon include quiche and meat pie.

From the hotel it's an easy drive to such famous spots as Bath, Stratford, and Oxford and to surrounding villages with such melodious names as Stow-on-the-Wold and Bourton-on-the-Water. As Heathrow Airport is only an hour and a half away, Lords of the Manor would be a memorable place to spend a last night in England. For guests staying five days, the fifth day is free.

Managers: Gabrielle and Anthony de Trafford. *Closed:* Two weeks in mid-January. *Recreational facilities:* Trout fishing at the hotel; golf a short drive away. *Facilities for children:* Baby-listening and playground. *Other facilities:* Drawing room, TV room, cocktail bar, garden. *Rooms:* 15 with bath and telephone. 2 ground-floor rooms. 5-day reduction; reduction for children under 10; winter breaks; Christmas program. No children under 2. Moderate to expensive. *Restaurant service:* Luncheon, snacks, dinner. *Credit cards:* Amex, Diners, Master, Visa. *How to get there:* Upper Slaughter is signposted on Route B4068 west of Stow-on-the-Wold. The hotel will meet guests at the train in Moreton-in-Marsh and will arrange for rental of self-drive or chauffeur-driven cars. *Telephone:* (0451) 20243.   [T]

LEEMING COUNTRY HOUSE

> I wandered lonely as a cloud
> That floats on high o'er vales and hills,
> When all at once I saw a crowd,
> A host, of golden daffodils;
> Beside the lake, beneath the trees
> Fluttering and dancing in the breeze.
>
> *William Wordsworth,* 1807

It was at this 20-acre estate on the shores of Lake Ullswater, that Wordsworth saw the daffodils that inspired his captivating poem. Each spring they dance and flutter there still. Of several suggestions for dining we gave to friends who rented a house in Cumbria, this was their favorite. "Very, very elegant, with delicious food" was their report.

Elegant indeed is this patrician Georgian mansion, its handsome appointments and lofty ceilings ornamented with elaborate plaster moldings. The atmosphere is that of a gracious, informal country house — a happy place with a young and friendly staff. Some bedrooms are in a modern addition. Whether you get an old or new room, ask for one facing the lake. A single room is just half the price of a double.

Proprietors: Mr. and Mrs. Fitzpatrick. *Closed:* December to mid-March. *Recreational facilities:* Fishing at the hotel; riding, sailing, and boat trips a short drive away. *Other facilities:* TV room, drawing room, library, cocktail bar, garden. *Rooms:* 24 with bath and telephone. Suitable for wheelchair guests. Off-season rates; 3-day reduction; winter breaks. No children under 8. Expensive to very expensive. *Restaurant service:* Luncheon, snacks, tea, dinner. *Credit cards:* Amex, Diners, Master, Visa. *How to get there:* The hotel is on Route A592 on the western shore of Lake Ullswater. *Telephone:* (08536) 622. *Agent in the United States:* Scott Calder. [T]

Welland, Hereford and Worcester

HOLDFAST COTTAGE

> This admirable region is a compendium of the general
> physiognomy of England.
>
> *Henry James,* 1875

For the traveler who values old-fashioned homeyness and good value
more than hotel luxury, this wisteria-covered cottage will be a delightful

find. Copper beech trees line the drive; garden furniture is sprinkled about under specimen trees on 2 acres of lawn and garden. Morning coffee and afternoon tea are offered there to the passerby as well as to house guests. Attractive rooms hold Oriental rugs, leather seating, Victorian bar chairs, and welcoming fires. Bedrooms are low-beamed and slanted (mind the head), all up a step here, down a step there, with pretty matching spreads and wallpaper. A table d'hôte dinner with three choices is served each evening with vegetables just picked from the Beetlestones' garden.

Prosperous farmlands surround this former farm cottage built more than three hundred years ago. The Malvern music festivals are close by, as are the Royal Worcester and Boehm porcelain factories.

Proprietors: Dennis and Diana Beetlestone. *Recreational facilities:* Outdoor and indoor pools, tennis, squash, riding, hunting, boat rental, and trips on the Upton and Severn rivers a short drive away. *Other facilities:* TV lounge, cocktail bar, garden. *Rooms:* 8 with bath and tea-making. Discount for children sharing; winter breaks; 3-day Christmas program. Inexpensive. *Restaurant service:* Tea, dinner. *How to get there:* The hotel is on Route A4104 between Little Malvern and Welland. *Telephone:* (0684) 310288. [T]

Wells, Somerset

CROWN HOTEL

> Wells is ideally situated...you come upon that glorious
> Cathedral, set amid surely the most beautiful Close that
> exists...a marvelous spot, civilized with the culture of
> centuries, yet quite unlike other cathedral towns.
>
> *George Gissing,* 1894

Wells is one of our favorite places in England. Of the many old hostelries clustered in its center near the cathedral, we liked the Crown best. It was built as an inn for pilgrims, but today most furnishings are modern yet tasteful, with antique accents here and there. There are mullioned windows and beams in bedrooms, some with four-poster beds. Try for one from which you can see the floodlit cathedral at night.

An old stone fireplace crackles a welcome in the entrance lounge, where guests can drink their after-dinner coffee. We enjoyed excellent roast lamb and broiled salmon as our main courses in the à la carte restaurant. Sautéed shrimp for an appetizer and old-fashioned bread pudding were also good choices. The friendly staff gave attentive service.

Before he came to America to found Pennsylvania in the seventeenth century, William Penn was arrested for speaking from a window of the Crown to the people below on Market Place, Quakers not being allowed to preach at that time. Every Wednesday and Saturday a market is still held there. From it we brought home a blue and white china teapot. We cherish a barometer we bought in an antique shop across from the Crown, more because it reminds us of captivating Wells than for the beautiful instrument itself.

Managers: Norman Evans and Michael Laurence. *Facilities:* Lounge, cocktail bar, laundry service, garden. *Rooms:* 14 with bath, telephone, TV, and tea-making. Breaks. Moderate. *Restaurant service:* Luncheon, snacks, dinner. *Credit cards:* Amex, Diners, Master, Visa. *How to get there:* The hotel is on Market Place in the center of Wells. *Telephone:* (0749) 78877.

West Witton, North Yorkshire

WENSLEYDALE HEIFER

> West Witton . . . a long struggle of houses nestling beneath the hill . . . on the right is a nice little pub, the Wensleydale Heifer, where Helen and I have had many meals over the years . . . we also stayed overnight.
> *James Herriot*

The Wensleydale Heifer was used by the cast and crew of the television series *All Creatures Great and Small*, based on the books by James Herriot. It is in his country, the setting for his delightful books.

On a crisp May morning, more like New England fall than English spring, we drove up, up, up twisting roads to find the horses at their morning gallops. The stable lads—and a "lad" can be fifty or she can be a girl—from the many training stables about, work out the beautiful animals on the great sweeps of uninterrupted lonely heath. It is a magnificent sight. We arrived in sunshine, but by the time the horses were cantering home, rain started, then sleet. Was it just the wind, or did I hear a faint cry, "Heeeathcliff"? Suddenly the sun again, and a rainbow stretched above the little villages clustered far below. This is one of our favorite memories of England.

This inn is the nearest to the high moors. In the bar it is easy to talk with local people who drop in. The attractive dining room is a recent addition to the seventeenth-century inn. The menu is extensive and the food delicious, attracting customers from cities not far away. Ask for a room at the back, as early-morning traffic is heavy through the village. One room has a four-poster bed.

Proprietors: John and Anne Sharp. *Recreational facilities:* River swimming a short walk away; riding and golf a short drive away. *Other facilities:* Lounge, public bar. *Rooms:* 17, 14 with bath, all with TV and tea-making. Ground-floor rooms. Breaks; 3-day Christmas and 2-day New Year's programs; free for children under 12 sharing. Inexpensive to moderate. *Restaurant service:* Early and late snacks and dinner. *Credit cards:* Diners, Master, Visa. *How to get there:* The inn is in the village on Route A684, a few miles west of Leyburn. *Telephone:* (0969) 22322. *Agent in the United States:* Consort Hotels.

Westonbirt, Gloucestershire

HARE AND HOUNDS

And every soul is welcome
That deigns to sojourn there
Samuel Waddington, 1844

The original inn dates from the early part of the last century, and the main hotel building was added in 1928, maintaining the old style. At that time the game of polo was much played at Westonbirt, and a suite of rooms was built to accommodate a famous maharaja who played it. Dining is in the baronial manner in the imposing restaurant overlooking the gardens, which are especially glorious with flowering fruit trees in springtime.

A few minutes' walk away is the beautiful Westonbirt Arboretum, with perhaps the finest collection of trees in Europe on its 161 acres. Included among the rare trees and shrubs imported from all over the world are magnificent specimens from America. In October the maples flame as they do in New England. Walks and drives are signposted throughout, and winter-flowering shrubs ensure year-round color.

This fine hotel is well decorated with many antiques and is warmed by log fires. What better place to end the day in could tired travelers find?

Proprietors: Jeremy and Martin Price. *Recreational facilities:* Tennis and squash at the hotel. *Facilities for children:* Baby-listening, children's meals. *Other facilities:* 2 lounges, game room, cocktail bar, public bar, garden. *Rooms:* 27, 23 with bath, all with telephone, TV, and tea-making. Breaks; Christmas program; free for children under 16 sharing. Inexpensive to moderate. *Restaurant service:* Luncheon, snacks, tea, dinner. *Credit cards:* Amex, Master, Visa. *How to get there:* The hotel is on Route A433, 2½ miles south of Tetbury and 1 mile north of Westonbirt village. *Telephone:* (066 688) 233. *Agent in the United States:* Best Western. [T]

Weybourne, Norfolk

MALTINGS HOTEL

The Village Inn, Sir, is a pleasant place
Where man finds company, good ale and grace,
And warmth when life is blowing cold outside
And that nice feeling—that these things abide.

John Nicholas

In a sturdy sixteenth-century flint building, a type of architecture typical of the area, the Maltings Hotel is the most attractive inn of the many we saw on the north Norfolk coast. Set near the sea but protected by a barrier range of sandy hills, it is decorated in a happy blend of old and new, using many antiques and appealing fabrics. The atmosphere is congenial and attentive, with such little extras offered as a newspaper of your choice delivered to your room each morning.

A large à la carte menu is presented in a rather formal dining room,

with crisp white linen and fine service, that has won culinary awards. On the hotel grounds stands the original maltsters' mash house, which is now a bar and buttery, well liked by both hotel guests and those who live in the neighborhood. Salads and a wide selection of fresh-caught seafood are always available.

Weybourne is within easy reach of the Norfolk Broads, a great haunt of wildfowl, and Sandringham Palace. Gourmets might want to have a meal at the highly lauded Gasche's Swiss restaurant in the village.

Proprietor: Ross Mears. *Recreational facilities:* Ocean swimming, tennis, riding, pheasant shooting, boat rental, and boat trips a short drive away. *Other facilities:* Lounge, library, cocktail bar, public bar, garden. *Rooms:* 23, 16 with bath, all with TV. Suitable for wheelchair guests. Off-season rates; Christmas program; breaks; children under 16 free sharing. Moderate. *Restaurant service:* Luncheon, early and late snacks, tea, dinner. *Credit cards:* Amex, Diners, Master, Visa. *How to get there:* The hotel is on Route A149 in Weybourne, between Blakeney and Cromer. The hotel will meet guests at the train in Sheringham (3 miles) or at the airport in Norwich. *Telephone:* (026 370) 275.

Whitwell on the Hill, North Yorkshire

WHITWELL HALL

Who can tell the pleasures of fancy when fancy takes her ease in an old English country-house, while the twilight darkens the corners of expressive rooms, and the appreciative intruder, pausing at the window . . . sees the great soft billows of the lawn melt away into the park?

Henry James, 1877

If your taste runs to luxurious country-house hotels, but your budget orders something less expensive, you might splurge for a night or two at

Whitwell Hall. Although its lowest-priced rooms in a converted coach house are not as elaborate as those in the main hall, they are comfortable. Staying in one will allow you to enjoy this beautiful estate at a most reasonable price.

The ivy-mantled Gothic-revival mansion is romantic. In the two-story great hall a striking cantilevered staircase ascends to an encircling balcony from which bedrooms open. Spacious rooms feature pointed stone arches, fine antique furnishings, oil paintings, and log fires. Cuisine is of a high standard, using meat and game produced locally, and fish from a nearby trout farm and the seacoast.

Visitors can play on tennis court and putting green and rove through 18 acres including terraced lawns, woodlands of yew, oak, and beech trees, rose beds, and a walled garden with lawn furniture and an ancient sundial. Bicycles are provided for exploring this beautiful part of North Yorkshire, and the Milners will arrange games of golf, tennis, and squash whenever possible.

Proprietors: Lieutenant Commander and Mrs. Peter Milner. *Recreational facilities:* Indoor pool, sauna, tennis, and putting green at the hotel; riding, hunting, squash, and golf a short drive away. *Other facilities:* Drawing room, great hall, cocktail bar, garden. *Rooms:* 21 with bath, some with telephone; TV available. No children under 13. 2-day reduction; breaks October through April; Christmas program. Moderate. *Restaurant service:* Dinner. *Credit cards:* Amex, Diners, Master, Visa. *How to get there:* The hotel is signposted on Route A64 northeast of York. *Telephone:* (065 381) 551. *Agent in the United States:* Romantik Hotels.   [T]

SWAN HOUSE HOTEL

> I'm a Warwickshire man . . . I know the *heart* of England. It has a hedgy, warm bountiful dimpled air. . . . Baby fields run up and down the little hills, and all the roads wriggle with pleasure.
>
> *Rupert Brooke,* 1913

The village of Shakespeare's mother, Mary Arden, is a peaceful place that doesn't suffer the throngs that fill the streets of Stratford-upon-Avon, 3 miles away. Those who are driving to Shakespeare land might well prefer to stay here, at the hospitable little Swan House Hotel that faces the village green. An entrance garden holds outdoor tables, a delightful place for a snack lunch or afternoon tea on a good day. You'll sit and look at timbered Mary Arden's Cottage, a stone's throw away.

The friendly bar doubles as a village pub where you will hear local gossip and can join the talk. In the very popular beamed and whitewashed dining room, you'll find a surprisingly full à la carte menu with salmon, lobster, goose, game, lamb, and steak and kidney pie frequently offered; there are always steak and duckling. The hotel is enhanced by an open log fire, old prints, and a few antiques. For a combination of fine food, cheerful service, and meticulous housekeeping, all at an extremely reasonable price, you'll be well pleased with the Swan House Hotel.

Proprietors: Pauline and Harry Poole. *Recreational facilities:* Riding a short walk away; tennis, squash, sauna, indoor pool, and golf a short drive away. *Other facilities:* Lounge, public bar, garden. *Rooms:* 11, 3 with bath, all with TV and tea-making. Breaks. Inexpensive. *Restaurant service:* Early and late snacks, tea, dinner. *Credit cards:* Amex, Master, Visa. *How to get there:* Take Route A34 from Stratford-upon-Avon. Turn left at the sign to Mary Arden's house. The hotel is at end of the street. The train stops nearby. *Telephone:* (0789) 67030.   [T]

Windermere, Cumbria

LANGDALE CHASE HOTEL

> I had the best view of Windermere . . . I think there can
> hardly be anything more beautiful in the world.
> *Nathaniel Hawthorne,* 1854

The entrance lounge is marvelous, a great hall two stories high. Its walls are early Tudor paneling, and a magnificent oak chimneypiece bears the date 1664 and is inscribed "Nicholas Tufton, Earl of Thanet, and Elizabeth, Countess of Thanet." Both the paneling and the chimneypiece were taken from an earlier house when this stone-built Victorian lakeside mansion was erected in 1890.

Before one of the many glowing fireplaces we enjoyed the best afternoon tea we had in England: thin cucumber sandwiches, buttered toast, scones and jam, cookies, raisin cake—the lot. It was all so delectably British, with the peaceful air of another era.

From the hotel's pier you can swim, water-ski, or row. You can stay in a unique bedroom in the boat house built out over the lake, drifting to sleep to the sound of lapping lake water. Inside the mansion the rooms

are a mélange of mosaic floors, oak balustrades, stained glass, tapestry, and velvet.

The grounds were laid out by the architect responsible for the Palace of Peace gardens in The Hague. Color abounds in the rose gardens, annual borders, flowering shrubs, and fine trees. From the stone terrace and cushioned bay windows there are some of the most dramatic views in Britain. Lawns slope to Lake Windermere, and across the lake wave upon wave of distant mountains seem to fall away into the mist.

Manager: Mrs. Frank. *Recreational facilities:* Lake swimming, water-skiing, rowboats, and tennis at the hotel; lake-steamer trips and riding a short drive away. *Other facilities:* Drawing room, TV lounge, cocktail bar, garden. *Rooms:* 34, 30 with bath, all with telephone, TV, and tea-making. Suitable for wheelchair guests. 2-day breaks; discount for children under 12 sharing. Moderate. *Restaurant service:* Luncheon, tea, dinner. *Credit cards:* Amex, Diners, Master, Visa. *How to get there:* The hotel is north of the town center on the road bordering Lake Windermere. It will meet trains at Windermere station. *Telephone:* (0966) 32201.

MILLER HOWE

My heart was almost melted away by the beauty of the lakes.

Dorothy Wordsworth, 1793

John Tovey, Miller Howe's entertaining host, loves to pamper his guests. He won the British Wine and Food Society award for the "outstanding meal of the year" and has received kudos from Craig Claiborne. John was an actor, and everything about the hotel is a little bit theatrical in a most joyous, friendly, and relaxing way. He told us, "A meal is like a play—every act something to look forward to." Meals here include many courses. Everyone sits down at eight-thirty each evening. The lights dim; the show begins.

The furnishings in the splendidly comfortable rooms are modern but not ordinary—great leather Chesterfield-type sofas and chairs are prominent—but the walls and tables brim with antique clutter. The bedrooms, hospitably supplied with not only books and current magazines but even binoculars, open to balconies overhanging terraces with stunning views of the lakeland that inspired so many of England's famous poets. Flower gardens display whimsical stone statuary.

All guests book for bed, full breakfast (bacon, sausage, kidneys, fresh eggs, tomatoes, mushrooms, kippers, finnan haddie, hot rolls), and dinner. This luxurious lodging is one that the seasoned collector of unusual hotels will not want to miss.

Proprietor: John Tovey. *Closed:* January—early March. *Recreational facilities:* Lake swimming at the hotel; riding, hunting, golf, and lake-fishing a short drive away. *Other facilities:* 4 lounges, garden. *Rooms:* 13 with bath. No children under 12. Expensive to very expensive. *Restaurant service:* Tea, dinner (by reservation). *Credit cards:* Amex, Diners, *How to get there:* Leave the M6 at exit 36 and proceed on Route A591 through Windermere. Turn left on Route A592 toward Bowness. The hotel is down a hill on the right. Guests can be met at the Manchester airport or at the Windermere railway station. *Telephone:* (09662) 2536.

BURGHOPE MANOR

> What delightful features in the landscape are those old-time England homes, built in the days when building was a living art...dear to the heart of antiquaries for the histories and traditions that have collected around their ancient walls!
> *James Hissey,* 1889

Burghope Manor is over 700 years old and has been in the Berysford family since shortly after it was built. Elizabeth Denning is a descendant of that family, which has the oldest recorded family name in England. By the time this oldest manor in Wiltshire came to her, years of neglect made expensive restoration imperative.

Elizabeth had worked in a hotel in the West Indies and missed it. She is also a very good cook. John is outgoing and hospitable. They decided to take paying guests but were determined to provide the kind of atmosphere friends create for friends. Says John, "People expect the British to be terribly formal, but they aren't like that with friends. That's how we see our guests. These old houses have been social gathering places for centuries, with a tradition of good conversation and a great deal of fun."

Usually, up to a dozen guests gather in a thirteenth-century dining room for dinner with their hosts, who sometimes invite local friends to join in. They all have drinks first in front of a roaring log fire, and conversation continues in the drawing room later over brandy and coffee. However, as good restaurants abound, the Dennings recommend that guests eat out some nights. English people frequently come to relax and play golf. If you can stay just one night, ask about dinner when you book your room. We hope you'll be there for a dinner party, but if your schedule won't allow it, you'll love staying in this beautiful home anyway. Breakfast is served informally whenever you come downstairs.

Two-and-a-half-acres of garden surround the low-slung house of pale Cotswold stone mantled in ivy. Inside is a wealth of arched Tudor doorways, wonderful beams that include ship's timbers in one bathroom, an Elizabethan stairway, a priest's hiding hole, and enormous fireplaces with mantels more than head high. Thomas Cranmer, archbishop to Henry VIII, was a guest at Burghope. Family tradition has it that a faint Latin inscription engraved on a stone chimney-piece was inscribed there by the Archbishop himself: "Remember the Sabbath and All that's holy. Six days shalt thou labour..." —the opening words, translated, of Cranmer's Church of England Prayer Book, commissioned by the king.

Surprisingly, the house is bright and airy, decorated with pastel colors. Light streams through large leaded-glass windows and French doors into a rose-carpeted drawing room. Bedrooms are pretty, with lovely floral fabrics. The modern bathrooms represent a marvelous change wrought by time.

We suggest that you stay here while you tour the beautiful but confusing nearby city of Bath. The Dennings will help you with maps and brochures of what to see. Burghope Manor offers a travel experience previously enjoyed by only a privileged few. The courtesy and hospitality with which we were treated are a happy memory yet.

Proprietors: Elizabeth and John Denning. *Recreational facilities:* Tennis at the house; golf nearby. *Other facilities:* Drawing room, sitting room, garden. *Rooms:* 6 with bath and tea-making. New Year's party. Not suitable for children. Expensive. *Credit card:* Amex. *How to get there:* From Route A36 take B3108 into Winsley, where you will see a 30 mph speed sign. Immediately after passing this, turn left onto a lane marked "Except for access." On the left is the high boundary wall of Burghope Manor. Follow it to the manor gate. *Telephone:* (022 122) 3557.

Woodstock, Oxfordshire

BEAR

> The Bear is an ancient inn, large and respectable, with balustraded staircases and intricate passages and corridors, and queer old pictures and engravings.
>
> *Nathaniel Hawthorne,* 1855

This is the kind of English inn you always hoped to find. It had already been dispensing hospitality for more than five hundred years when Queen Anne bestowed the Royal Manor of Woodstock on the first duke of Marlborough in 1704, as a reward for his victory at Blenheim. There he

built the enormous Blenheim Palace, where one of his famous descendants, Sir Winston Churchill, was born — but only because his mother was visiting at the time; his branch of the family had not inherited Blenheim or the title. It was later home to young Consuelo Vanderbilt, pressed against her wishes by an ambitious, determined mother to marry the then duke of Marlborough in 1895. Her autobiography, *The Glitter and the Gold*, describes her life at Blenheim.

The Bear, in a quiet country town, has many associations with kings and queens of the past, as Woodstock was the site of one of the royal courts of England. Today you can enjoy the same atmosphere that through the centuries brought famous personalities as visitors, and more recently the Burtons — Richard and Elizabeth — and the late Vice-President Nelson Rockefeller.

The Bear is one of the finest of the original coaching inns. It is commended by just about everyone who has visited it.

Manager: Michael Porter. *Special facilities:* Lounge, cocktail bar, public bar. *Rooms:* 45, 37 with bath, all with TV and telephone. Suitable for wheelchair guests. 2-day breaks; discount for children. Very expensive. *Restaurant service:* Luncheon, snacks, dinner. *Credit cards:* All. *How to get there:* Woodstock is on Route A34 about 8 miles north of Oxford. *Telephone:* (0993) 811 511. *Agent in the United States:* Ray Morrow.   [T]

York, North Yorkshire

BOOTHAM BAR HOTEL

We . . . took a promenade along the wall, and a ramble through some of the crooked streets, noting the old jutting storied house . . . gnawed like a bone by the teeth of time.

Nathaniel Hawthorne, 1854

The Bootham Bar is a small hotel in a superb location by the Minster (cathedral) and next to the Bootham Bar Gate of the medieval wall. In our third-floor bedroom we were startled to hear voices outside our window. We looked out to see schoolchildren just a few yards away, walking along the high, ancient wall that rings the old city. Before breakfast next morning we, too, climbed the worn stone steps near the front door of the hotel, transporting ourselves into another age. A parapet 6 feet high, with narrow openings for archers to defend the city, is along the outside of the wide path that tops the wall. Below is a moat, and beyond it are the traffic and houses of the modern city. Along the other edge a waist-high stone fence protects the walkway but allows delightful views of the lawns and gardens of the Deanery and other ancient houses that were built in the shadow of the cathedral.

Centuries crowded with events have made York a rich tapestry of the past. We walked down the street to the attractive Young's restaurant in the house where Guy Fawkes, who tried to blow up Parliament, was born in 1570. Lunch was so good we returned for dinner.

Just think of the streams of people over the centuries who have passed through the Bootham Bar; knights in chain mail on armored horses, weary foot travelers in hose and jerkin, farmers in wooden-wheeled carts, and later the elite of the roads in the glamorous coaching age. On the Bootham Bar this notice is posted: "In olden times armed men were stationed here to watch and to conduct travellers through the forest and protect them against wolves."

The Bootham Bar Hotel serves no meals except breakfast and has no liquor license.

Proprietors: John and Beverly Dearnly. *Closed:* A few days for Christmas. *Special facilities:* Lounge, garden. *Rooms:* 8 with bath, TV, and tea-making. Inexpensive. *How to get there:* The hotel is at 4 High Petergate. *Telephone:* (0904) 58516.

We would like to hear about your experiences. If you have comments, suggestions, or recommendations about these or other inns and historic hotels, please write to us, Eileen and Eugene O'Reilly, c/o Burt Franklin & Co., Inc., 235 East 44th St., New York, New York 10017 U.S.A.

SCOTLAND

LEDGOWAN LODGE HOTEL

> Regions mountainous and wild, thinly inhabited, and little cultivated, make a great part of the earth, and he that has never seen them must live unacquainted with much of the face of nature.
>
> *Samuel Johnson,* 1775

Everything about this former shooting lodge evokes an aura of Edwardian expansiveness. A roomy reception lounge has mounted stags' heads on the wall, all shot on the estate, and a fire on the hearth. In the dining room, three crystal chandeliers are reflected in the 10-foot-high mirror backing a Victorian serving buffet that takes up most of one wall. It's easy to imagine portly Edward VII and his cronies puffing on cigars while lingering over port wine here. Vension is on the menu when available; we enjoyed roast turkey and cranberry, served in the Scottish fashion with bacon. In a lounge full of big overstuffed sofas and chairs, 18-inch solid brass sash lifts are used to open the large bay windows.

A wainscoted stair, with a bust of Queen Victoria and a stained-glass window on the landing, sweeps upstairs. One of the hall bathrooms there contains a colossal tub, which looked almost too high to climb into, and a long marble washstand. The room's pièce de résistance was the vast mahogany seat atop a flowered blue and white china bowl, a wooden toilet tank with pull-chain high above it: all in perfect working order. This masterpiece is one of a kind, however; other bathrooms are modern. Bedrooms command views of austere mountain scenery.

Graham Millard, the genial host, owns 10 acres of what was the 8,500-acre Ledgowan estate. The lodge—a place of cheerful, solid comfort, not fancy, with a warm, friendly atmosphere, central heat, and electric blankets—offers very good value in the sparsely inhabited western Highlands.

Proprietors: Graham and Sheila Millard. *Closed:* November through March. *Facilities:* Lounge, TV lounge, cocktail bar, gift shop, garden. *Rooms:* 15, 9 with bath, all with tea-making. Three-day reduction; free for children under 16 sharing. Inexpensive to moderate. *Restaurant service:* Luncheon, snacks, tea, dinner. *Credit cards:* Amex, Diners, Master, Visa. *How to get there:* The hotel is on Route A832 west of Garve. *Telephone:* (044 588) 252. *Agent in the United States:* Best Western. [T]

LOCH DUICH HOTEL

> This day's journey was through fine wild Highland
> scenery, where rocks...were tumbled upon each other,
> as if by giants in a passion.   *Maria Edgeworth,* 1823

After traveling through fine, wild Highland scenery, we sat in a sunny
living room in a wayside inn on the road to the Isle of Skye. We were
looking out at picturesque Eilean Donan's Castle, which you may have
seen on Scottish Tourist Board posters. As the pub was not open, we
were having a snack lunch on a tray in this pleasant room with flowered-
cretonne-covered chairs. Such a cheerful inn it was, where friendly Scottish hospitality marked the service. On a windy spring day we were enjoying hotchpotch, a traditional mutton broth thickened with a rich variety
of spring vegetables.

For generations Eilean Donan's Castle was a stronghold of the
MacRae clan's. In 1719 it was garrisoned by Spanish troops who came to
support the Old Pretender, James III, and it was battered by an English
warship. On an islet in the loch, connected to the shore by a short
causeway, the castle is now restored as a Jacobite museum and a
memorial to the MacRaes. It is a short, pleasant walk from the hotel.

While we were at lunch, through the window we saw a van drive up to
the hotel, open up, and put stairs out for villagers, who began to climb in
and out. We investigated and found it to be a mobile bank, and we
cashed some traveler's checks. Mobile banks are necessary in this sparsely
populated land. The hotel is the center for this tiny village. A bar with a
separate outside entrance is the village pub, and we were surprised to find
a beauty salon on the hotel grounds.

We were advised that the loch swimming here is for strong swimmers
only, but the Loch Duich Hotel is a happy haven on a tour of the western
Highlands.

Proprietors: Rod and Geraldine Stenson. *Closed:* November through
March. *Recreational facilities:* Loch swimming, riding, and boat trips
nearby. *Other facilities:* Living room, public bar, hairdresser. *Rooms:* 18
with shared baths; 2-day reduction; reduction for children sharing. Inexpensive. *Restaurant service:* Snacks, tea, dinner. *How to get there:* The
hotel is on Route A87, some 8 miles east of Kyle of Lochalsh, where the
ferry leaves for the Isle of Skye. Buses stop at the hotel. *Telephone:* (059
985) 213.   [T]

ASPEN HOTEL

> Worship for members of the Royal Family is probably
> carried to greater lengths at Ballater than anywhere else
> in a loyal kingdom. Even the Prince Consort is still
> revered in Ballater, and no one in this town has ever been
> heard to utter a word against the Albert Memorial.
>
> *H. V. Morton,* 1930

"By Appointment to Her Majesty the Queen." The bakery shop owned
by the Murdochs bears the royal commendation. If you are their guests at
the Aspen Hotel, you'll enjoy the same bread and pastries that are served
at the royal table. Right on the main street of the famous town, this
modest little hotel—guest house would seem a more appropriate term for
it—is a find for the budget traveler. Decorating is plain but cheerful.

This whole area is haunted by the shadow of a little old lady in black,
clip-clopping along the roads in a basket cart pulled by a Shetland pony.
The grounds of Balmoral Castle are open May through July, except Sundays and when the royal family is in residence.

Proprietors: William and Irene Murdoch. *Closed:* November
through March. *Recreational facilities:* Putting green at the hotel; tennis,
squash, river swimming, riding, and golf nearby. *Facilities for children:*
Baby-sitting. *Other facilities:* Lounge, TV lounge, garden. *Rooms:* 13, 4
with bath and TV, all with tea-making. Ground-floor room. Discount for
children under 14. Very inexpensive. *How to get there:* The hotel is on the
main road in Ballater. *Telephone:* (0338) 55486.

TULLICH LODGE

> To me, not the least delight of travel is the ever-growing
> picture-gallery of beauty spots that I gather and treasure
> in my mind.   *James Hissey,* 1910

Tullich Lodge is a beauty spot. The nineteenth-century baronial mansion
of pink granite is surrounded by 5 acres of garden and woodland that
command lovely views over Royal Deeside. The rooms are furnished with
antiques, fine fabrics, and flowers, assembled with style and maintained
to perfection. A unique piece is the Edwardian glass telephone booth in
the hall. If you don't mind the climb, there is a romantic tower bedroom

with a panoramic outlook.

The food is served according to a set menu. No lesser a critic than Craig Claiborne, in singing its praises, has said that the breads were the best he had in Scotland, which, he thought, had some of the world's best breads. Roast lamb and beef are popular, and you can get yours pink, a hue not always available where meat is served in Britain. If you stay two nights and take dinner, the rate per night is hardly more than the bed-and-breakfast rate for one night.

The grounds of neighboring Balmoral Castle are open in May, June, and July, except on Sundays and when the royal family is in residence.

Proprietors: Hector Macdonald and Neil Bannister. *Closed:* December through March. *Recreational facilities:* Golf, tennis, and river swimming nearby. *Other facilities:* Drawing room, sitting room, cocktail bar, garden. *Rooms:* 10 with bath. 2-day reduction; reduction for children sharing. Expensive to very expensive. *Restaurant service:* Luncheon, snacks, dinner (by reservation), children's supper. *Credit card:* Amex. *How to get there:* The hotel is signposted 1 mile east of Ballater on Route A93. *Telephone:* (0338) 55406. *Agent in the United States:* Abercrombie and Kent. [T]

BANCHORY LODGE

Land of my high endeavor,
Land of the shining river,
Land of my heart forever,
Scotland the brave.

C. Hanley

The glory of Banchory Lodge is its setting where the Feugh flows into the River Dee, one of the most celebrated salmon rivers in Britain. You'll be lulled to sleep by the music of its tumbling waters, and in spring you can watch salmon leaping the rapids.

The white Georgian mansion, built in 1738 for the Burnett Ramsays, was later the retirement home of an equerry to King George IV. Then, as a coaching inn, it knew the shouts of ostlers and postboys. Today's fine hotel is heavily patronized by fishermen, but unless you reserve in advance and bring gear, don't plan to catch any salmon or trout.

An ideal spot for the armchair fisherman is a big chintz-covered chair in the beautiful lounge that looks out on the churning of the two merging rivers. The Jaffrays have collected old treasures over the years, including two four-posters, to furnish the rooms. Fresh flowers are everywhere, inside and out. Fresh Deeside salmon and Aberdeen Angus roast beef are specialties in the highly praised dining room, which has another fine view of the river. For year-round comfort there are log fires in lounges and bar and electric blankets, as well as central heat. The area is one of the driest in Scotland. This superior hotel is always well filled; so book ahead.

Proprietors: Dugald and Margaret Jaffray. *Closed:* Mid-December through January. *Recreational facilities:* Sauna at the hotel; tennis and squash a short walk away. *Facilities for children:* Baby-listening. *Other facilities:* Lounge, TV lounge, cocktail bar, garden. *Rooms:* 25 with bath, TV, and tea-making. Ground-floor room. 3-day reduction; reduction for children under 10. Moderate to expensive. *Restaurant service:* Luncheon, tea, dinner (jacket and tie required). *Credit cards:* Amex, Visa. *How to get there:* The inn is signposted on Route A93 in Banchory, which is between Aberdeen and Braemar. *Telephone:* (033 02) 2625.   [T]

Callander, Central

HIGHLAND HOUSE HOTEL

I always, when possible, seek out some house of entertainment conducted upon personal lines, if on a less palatial scale, and where some sort of local atmosphere is floating about.

Arthur Bradley, 1903

On a pretty street in the town of Callander, little Highland House is conducted along personal lines by Eslyn and David Craven. Their children help out too. Eslyn, a trained cook, produces an à la carte menu from local produce that includes some traditional Scottish dishes, home-made soups, and tempting desserts. David works as a land agent and surveyor, helping at the house in the evening and on weekends. This is the sort of place where many an enjoyable evening is spent in conversation around a log fire.

Although the life of the small town is but a block or two away to the left as you step out the front door, just down the street in the opposite direction is beautiful countryside for walking, from easy walks through glens for an hour or so to full-day hill excursions for dedicated hikers. This small hotel, run by well-traveled owners, will be a happy find for those seeking inexpensive lodgings.

Proprietors: Eslyn and David Craven. *Closed:* November through February. *Recreational facilities:* Tennis, squash, golf, trout and salmon fishing, and boat rental a short walk away; riding, loch swimming, and boat trips a short drive away. *Facilities for children:* Baby-sitting and -listening. *Other facilities:* TV lounge, cocktail lounge, garden. *Rooms:* 10, 4 with bath. Off-season rates; reduction for children. Very inexpensive to inexpensive. *Restaurant service:* Dinner. *How to get there:* Highland House is on South Church Street, which bisects the main street of Callander on Route A84 between Stirling and Lochearnhead. *Telephone:* (0877) 30269.

ROMAN CAMP HOTEL

> thou shalt find
> All that's generous, all that's kind.
> Friendship, virtue, every grace,
> Dwelling in this happy place.
>
> *Robert Burns*

All that's generous, all that's kind. It would be difficult not to be happy in this charming old hunting lodge built on the site of a Roman encampment. Twenty acres of gardens lush with color and fragrance are the setting for the pink-washed building, mellowed by over three hundred years. This haven of peace and beauty, with country-house atmosphere, is in the town of Callander, a walk away from shops in possibly the most popular inland resort in Scotland.

Antiques mingle with comfortable pieces in the rooms. Of particular interest is the dark paneling of the library and entrance hall and the tapestry-covered walls of the lounge. Bedrooms offer such nice extras as fresh flowers and fruit. Electric blankets insure that you'll be warm.

But the food here may be the main attraction. Swiss-born Sami Denzler ran a fine restaurant in Edinburgh, where we had the best dinners of a trip to Scotland a few years back. Now, under the friendly ownership of Sami and his wife Pat, the fine reputation of the Roman Camp Hotel has been revived.

Proprietors: Samuel and Pat Denzler. *Closed:* Late November – mid-February. *Recreational facilities:* Tennis, squash, loch swimming, riding, and boat trips nearby. *Other facilities:* Lounge, sitting room, sun lounge, cocktail bar, library, laundry service, garden. *Rooms:* 11 with bath, telephone, TV, and tea-making; 1 suite. Ground-floor rooms. Moderate. *Restaurant service:* Dinner. *How to get there:* The hotel is on Route A84 in Callander. *Telephone:* (0877) 30003. *Agent in the United States:* Romantik Hotels. [T]

WHITE SHUTTERS

> So wondrous wild, and whole might seem
> The scenery of a fairy dream.
>
> *Sir Walter Scott,* 1810

Callander, although not wild itself, is known as the gateway to the Trossachs, an area immortalized by Sir Walter Scott in his romantic stories of Scotland. The opening scene of *The Lady of the Lake*, that favorite of high school English courses, takes place on the nearby moor. Time has left essentially unchanged the solitude that Dorothy Wordsworth called the "perfection of loveliness and beauty." It is still haunted by the ghosts of people who never lived—the figures of Scott's imagination.

White Shutters is a friendly guest house from which to tour the Trossachs. There can hardly be a more cheerful and helpful man in Scotland than host Jackie Dickinson. In the neat little house, which stands on a pretty street in the town center, modest rooms are simply furnished and meticulously kept. Except for breakfast, neither meals nor spirits are available; but Highland House is right next door, and other good restaurants are handy. Included in the room rate are evening tea and snacks, hospitably served in the lounge at ten o'clock. White Shutters was filmed by the BBC and shown on a TV program that presented different types of vacation options. It should delight any budget traveler.

Proprietors: Isobel and Jackie Dickinson. *Closed:* November through March. *Recreational facilities:* Tennis and squash a short walk away; loch swimming, riding, and boat trips a short drive away. *Other facilities:* TV lounge. *Rooms:* 4 sharing bath. Off-season rate; reduction for children. No children under 5. Very inexpensive. *How to get there:* White Shutters is on South Church Street, which bisects the main street of Callander, on Route A84 between Stirling and Lochearnhead. A bus will deposit you a few steps away. *Telephone:* (0877) 30442.

Connel, Strathclyde

FALLS OF LORA HOTEL

My heart's in the Highlands, I love every glen,
Every corrie and crag in the land of the Ben.
John Campbell

In peaceful, rolling farm country where shaggy cattle graze, we found this well-modernized 1886 hotel that offers many services at guest-house prices. A lot of Victorian charm has been retained in the mix of old and new furnishings—carved tables, paintings in heavy frames, a deer head high on a wall. Through bay windows in a lounge with big floral-covered chairs, there is a beautiful view across cultivated gardens to Loch Etive. In cold weather you'll be warm in a centrally heated section where each bedroom has both electric blankets and an electric heater, and log fires glow in the friendly bar.

The accent is on personal attention by the owners, who enjoy making you feel at home. Restaurant service is varied and extensive: The dinner menu offers good choices and hearty bar snacks, served all day and evening, include steak, chicken, and fish with French fries, shrimp cocktail, and desserts.

The hotel is especially good for train travelers. Connel station is just a few minutes' walk away, and a bus runs regularly the 5 miles to Oban, from where you can take boat trips to legendary Iona and others of the romantic Western Isles. The lower-priced rooms here are an exceptional value.

Proprietor: Catherine Webster. *Recreational facilities:* Boat rental, water-skiing, ocean swimming, indoor pool, tennis, squash, sauna, riding, boat trips to the islands, and gliding a short drive away. *Facilities for children:* Baby-listening. *Other facilities:* Lounge, TV lounge, cocktail bar, public bar, garden, laundry service. *Rooms:* 30, 15 with bath, TV in some. Suitable for wheelchair guests. Off-season rates; children free if sharing, otherwise a discount. Very inexpensive to moderate. *Restaurant service:* Luncheon, snacks all day and evening, tea, dinner. *Credit cards:* Amex, Diners, Master, Visa. *How to get there:* Connel is on Route A85, 5 miles north of Oban on the west coast of Scotland. The railroad station is near the hotel. *Telephone:* (0631 71) 483.   [T]

Cullen, Grampian

SEAFIELD ARMS

> Cullen has a snug, warm, comfortable appearance though but a very small town.
>
> *James Boswell,* 1773

When James Boswell toured Scotland with Sam Johnson in 1773, he found few attractive small towns. There are many more today, but the prosperous seaside town of Cullen, its small gray-stone houses trimmed with bright paint, still takes honors as one of the most appealing.

The Seafield Arms on Cullen's main street still welcomes travelers as it has since 1822, when it was built by the earl of Seafield. This fine old coaching inn has been skillfully decorated in fresh bright colors. A magnificent carved mantel that was once in a mansion takes pride of place in the luxurious cocktail bar. Chintz-covered chairs, bird prints, Sanderson fabrics and wallpapers, brass beds, are just a few of the nice touches throughout the inn. The dining room, carpeted with specially woven

Grant tartan, has long been famous for regional specialties: salmon, trout, grouse, pheasant, partridge, and Aberdeen Angus beef. Guests can have lunch in the sun on a protected terrace, pretty with white iron furniture and blue umbrellas, or in the Stable Bar, all stone and old wood, where local folk-groups entertain two or three nights a week.

Along the waterfront in Cullen are stone benches where you can sit and watch small boats come in to anchor behind a breakwater. A sandy beach with sand dunes behind it stretches alongside. Cullen House, home of the earl and countess of Seafield, is generally open during the summer, and the Old Kirk, one of the few pre-Reformation kirks in regular use, is worth a visit.

Proprietors: Mr. and Mrs. John Duguid. *Recreational facilities:* Ocean swimming and tennis a short walk away; indoor pool and riding a short drive away. *Facilities for children:* Baby-listening. *Other facilities:* Lounge, TV lounge, cocktail bar, public bar, terrace. *Rooms:* 23 with bath, TV, telephone and tea-making. Breaks; 3-day New Year's program; free for children under 12 sharing. Expensive. *Restaurant service:* Luncheon, snacks, high tea, dinner. *Credit cards:* Amex, Diners, Master, Visa. *How to get there:* Cullen is on Route A98 between Aberdeen and Inverness. *Telephone:* (0542) 40791.   [T]

THE OPEN ARMS

> Dirleton is assuredly a delectable little place. It mostly
> fronts upon a village green, one side of which is occupied
> by a hoary fortress of historic fame. An admirable old
> inn has the place of honour.
>
> *Arthur G. Bradley,* 1912

The admirable old inn still faces the green in lovely Dirleton. Today it is
bright and sunny, nicely decorated in a simple modern style. Most bedrooms are of average size, but number 10 is larger, with a bay window
overlooking the hoary fortress mentioned above, the romantic ruins of a
thirteenth-century castle.

The restaurant offers an imaginative menu with some Taste-of-
Scotland specialities. You might start your dinner with smoked trout
mousse or mussel and onion stew and end it with Flummery Drambui.
Room service is offered at no extra charge. Afternoon tea with Scottish
shortbread, enjoyed before a friendly fire in the lounge, is wonderfully
relaxing after a day of golf or sightseeing. The cocktail bar is popular
with locals and visitors alike.

There are seven golf courses within three miles of the hotel that are
open all year. Central heat and electric blankets will keep you warm all
winter, and two-day breaks from November to May are a bargain.

Proprietor: Arthur Neil. *Recreational facilities:* Golf, tennis, indoor
pool, ocean swimming, riding, boat rental, and boat trips nearby. *Other
facilities:* 2 lounges, cocktail bar, garden. *Rooms:* 7 with bath, telephone,
and TV. 3-day reduction; winter breaks; reduction for children. Moderate. *Restaurant service:* Luncheon, snacks, tea, dinner. *Credit cards:*
Amex, Diners, Visa. *How to get there:* Dirleton is 20 miles northeast of
Edinburgh on Route A198. *Telephone:* (062085) 241. *Agent in the United
States:* Josephine Barr. [T]

LEWISTON ARMS

> Wherever I wander, wherever I rove,
> The hills of the Highlands forever I love.
>
> *Robert Burns*

The ruin of Urquhart Castle, medieval home of the Grants, who were chiefs of the glens hereabouts, is on the banks of Loch Ness, just where sightings of the monster are most frequently reported. Within walking distance we found the Lewiston Arms, a homey inn whose visitors are soon friendly with the owners, Nicky and Helen Quinn. After driving through mountains, we were delighted to be given afternoon tea on the back lawn. We sat beside the River Coilty, which tumbles along its boulder-strewn bed into Loch Ness.

In the little cretonne-filled lounge, residents are bound to chat with one another and with guests who come in just for dinner. Helen's cooking is so good that it is recommended in the top British food guides. There is always fresh trout on the extensive menu, but duck à l'orange was our choice after a smoked haddock chowder and prawns, all topped off by homebaked apple tart. Bedrooms are small and functional. Nicky tends the taproom, the village pub, which is entered from the street. It provides a setting for camaraderie where travelers are welcome to join in the talk.

If you'd like to try to spot Nessie yourself, walk first to the Loch Ness Monster Exhibition, where not only photographs and a model of the monster but also underwater images taken with sonar and stroboscopic equipment will show you what to look for.

This modest little inn will not suit those who need spacious rooms, but we enjoyed its fine food and snug cheerfulness.

Proprietors: Nick and Helen Quinn. *Recreational facilities:* Riding a short walk away; boat trips a short drive away. *Other facilities:* Lounge, TV lounge, public bar, garden. *Rooms:* 8 sharing baths. Off-season rates; reduction for children. Very inexpensive. *Restaurant service:* Snacks, tea, dinner. *How to get there:* The hotel is on Route A82 between Fort William and Inverness. *Telephone:* (045 62) 225.

Dunkeld, Tayside

CARDNEY HOUSE

That man travels to no purpose who sits alone to his meals.

John Davis, 1802

Cardney House is a warm and elegant family home with the family still in it. Here the Laird and Mistress MacGregor will welcome you and treat you as a guest, not merely as a customer. In the informal house-party atmosphere, all visitors mix cordially.

The eighteenth-century manor is beautifully and comfortably appointed throughout. Decorating is light and airy. In some spacious bedrooms, painted furniture mixes well with family antiques. Flowers are everywhere. The laird, who is retired from the navy, has greenhouses where he grows orchids, stephanotis, and lemon and orange trees commercially. It's quite a thrill to awaken and see sprays of orchids in your bedroom's vases.

Mistress MacGregor, whom guests call Mariquita, cooks dinner herself but with such good management that she is able to dine with her guests. For the evening, women change to dresses, long or short, and men wear coat and tie. The laird may wear a kilt. Wine and other spirits are available. In fact, the whisky here is special. A huge cask is kept aging in the cellars. As some is drawn off the bottom, more is added to the top so the aging process is continuous.

There is usually a college-age girl acting as Mariquita's assistant, adding to the informal atmosphere. One of the requirements for the job is the ability to play tennis, as Mariquita likes to have someone to play with when no guests accommodate. Mariquita is a concert singer and has toured the United States. Sometimes there is music during the evening.

On the 2,000-acre estate, fallow and roe deer are abundant. From the dining-room window, we watched two come from the woods and hesitantly cross the lawn. Mariquita just wrote to us "We have been filmed for a 10-episode TV film, *King's Royal*, coming out at the end of the year. It will go to the USA later."

Many guests return to Cardney—one family, nine times in eight years. For us, it is a cherished memory and was our favorite stop in Scotland on our last trip.

Proprietors: Findanus and Mariquita MacGregor. *Recreational facilities:* Tennis at the house, shooting, stalking, and fishing arranged in season. *Other facilities:* Drawing room, sun lounge, garden. *Rooms:* 8 with bath. Elevator. 3-day reduction. Not suitable for children under 14. Inexpensive. *Restaurant service:* Dinner by reservation. *How to get there:* About 3 miles from Dunkeld on Route A923, toward Blairgowrie, on the left is a stone gatepost with "Cardney" carved on it. There is no other sign. Drive in. *Telephone:* (03504) 222.

GREENSIDE HOTEL

> A large, populous, nobel, rich and even still a royal city
> . . . the buildings are surprising both for strength and for
> beauty. . . . No blowing of tiles about the streets, to
> knock people on the head . . . as we often find it in
> London.
>
> *Daniel Defoe,* 1699

On a lovely curved crescent of joined Georgian houses, close to the American consulate, there is a friendly hotel for those seeking inexpensive lodging in Edinburgh. This convenient location is an energetic walk or one bus-stop from Princes Street and a ten-minute walk from the Waverley train station. Parking is in a metered city-parking area close to the hotel.

Terraced gardens behind the hotel are particularly attractive. They lead up into a private park that is entered only from the gardens behind all the houses on this crescent. From the park's height there are fine views over Edinburgh. Bathrooms at Greenside are all new, with both tub and shower. Some nice prints and the occasional antique piece are among the plainer furnishings. The hotel has no license to serve spirits.

Two other good, plain, inexpensive hotels are recommended in the same area. Park Hotel, at 32 Royal Terrace, is a bit more money but serves dinner and has a lounge and a bar as well as the TV lounge. It has twenty-six rooms, eight with private bath, and the same kind of terraced garden leading to the private park. Belmont Hotel, at 10 Carlton Terrace, has a resident's bar and one bedroom with a private bath, but doesn't have the garden. We found this section of Edinburgh to be the most attractive area with inexpensive hotels.

Proprietors: David and Dorothy Simpson. *Special facilities:* TV lounge, garden. *Rooms:* 10, 1 with bath. Off-season rates; reduction for children under 12 sharing. Inexpensive. *How to get there:* Greenside Hotel is at 9 Royal Terrace, off London Road, which is a continuation of Route A1. *Telephone:* (031) 557 0022.

THE HOWARD HOTEL

> They have begun to build what is to be called the New Town. The houses...are airy and handsome, built entirely in the *English* taste; so that each family are to enjoy a whole house to themselves.
>
> *Daniel Defoe,* 1719

Three handsome terrace houses, built in Edinburgh's New Town a century after Defoe saw its beginnings, were combined to become The Howard Hotel. An imposing staircase under a glass roof sweeps up to comfortable bedrooms. Some of these are furnished with antiques that include brass beds, while others are more modern.

Enjoy lunch in the mellow club-like atmosphere of The Claret Jug, a bar renowned for its delicious cold buffet (except on Sunday), which attracts local business people and residents. Candlelight and flowers complement good food served in a luxurious dining room.

This fine central hotel is small enough to offer personal service and has its own parking area. Great King Street is parallel to Princes Street five blocks away.

Proprietor: Mrs. Arthur Neil. *Facilities:* Lounge, public bar, cocktail bar, parking. *Rooms:* 25 with bath, telephone, TV, and tea-making. Reduction for children; winter breaks. Moderate to expensive. *Restaurant service:* Luncheon, snacks, dinner. *Credit cards:* Amex, Diners, Master, Visa. *Mailing address:* 32 Great King Street, Edinburgh EH3 6QH. *How to get there:* From the city center on Princes Street, turn down Hanover Street; go five blocks, turn right. The hotel is on the left. *Telephone:* (031 557) 3500. *Agent in the United States:* Josephine Barr. [T]

Fort William, Highland

INVERLOCHY CASTLE

At a quarter-past eight we left Inverlochy Castle, where
we had spent very pleasant days.

Queen Victoria, 1873

The quality of Inverlochy Castle matches the life-style and bestows on its
guests the attention to which the queen was accustomed, but without the

formality required in Victorian days. Guests gather together in the evening before fires in two luxurious lounges, where the atmosphere is reminiscent of pre-1914 country-house parties described in English novels. There is even a billiards room.

Dramatically set in the very shadow of Ben Nevis, Britain's highest mountain, the castle stands amid a striking collection of rhododendron in 50 acres of woods and gardens. Spacious rooms hold a wealth of antique furniture and Oriental rugs; masses of flowers are everywhere. Decorated with floral fabrics, the large nineteenth-century bedrooms provide the ultimate in twentieth-century comfort and offer dramatic mountain views. The dining room, which has won top honors in every British food guide, equals the quality of the rest of the castle, and the cellar includes the choicest wines. Just a few nonresident guests are seated at dinner, strictly by reservation.

Mrs. Hobbs takes a personal interest in her guests. She and her friendly staff cater to individual requirements. A chauffered limousine will meet guests at trains or airports and can be engaged for leisurely touring. Robert Redford, Larry Hagman, Charlie Chaplin, and ambassadors and other government officials have all stayed at Inverlochy. It is probably the most luxurious—and the most expensive— country inn in Britain. Happy visitors always say it is worth every penny. Those who have the pennies will find that there is just one word for it: marvelous!

Proprietor: Grete Hobbs. *Closed:* Mid-November—mid-March. *Recreational facilities:* Tennis and trout fishing at the hotel; riding, golf, boat rental, and boat trips a short drive away. *Other facilities:* Drawing room, lounge, billiards room, garden. *Rooms:* 16 with bath, TV, and telephone. Very expensive. *Restaurant service:* Luncheon, dinner (by reservation). *Credit cards:* Master, Visa. *How to get there:* The castle is signposted on Route A82, 3 miles north of Fort William. Guests can be met at the Fort William railway station or at airports in Glasgow and Edinburgh. *Telephone:* (0397) 2177.

Glenshiel, Highland

KINTAIL LODGE

> Hark when the night is falling,
> Hear! Hear the pipes are calling
> Loudly and proudly calling,
> Down thro' the glen.
>
> *C. Hanley*

The pipes can sometimes still be heard calling proudly down the glen under the Five Sisters of Kintail. These peaks are some of the loveliest mountains of Wester Ross, and beneath them is a wayside inn on the road to Skye.

We were told by our nephew and his Scottish wife not to miss Kintail Lodge, their favorite stop on a tour of the Highlands. We found it a relaxed, friendly place that captures the spirit of true Highland hospitality.

In a sprightly dining room that has red and white checked tablecloths, you will feast on homemade pâté and soups, home-baked bread and pastries. But don't think the food is simple home fare. A memorable dinner might start with haddock mousse or avocado with prawns. Then you could choose roast pheasant, Loch Duich salmon Doria, honey-baked pork with applesauce, or beef Wellington; and finish with a selection from the sweets trolley and cheese board.

A bar is also the village pub where local people come in to play pool under the gaze of an East African impala inherited from the hunting-lodge days. An attractive, homey lounge, with plenty of books and magazines about, holds some antique pieces that range from an inlaid grandfather clock to cane carpet-beaters displayed on a wall. Some bedrooms have inlaid furniture, others are done up with modern rustic pine. All are color-coordinated with pretty wallpapers, wall-to-wall carpeting, and continental quilts (central heating and electric blankets, too).

In summer you can take a rowboat or canoe right from the hotel to glide along the waters of Loch Duich. On brisk autumn days, explore the hill paths used by Highlands shepherds, then return to afternoon tea before an open fire. This is an especially good choice for those traveling off-season when many hotels in the remote Western Highlands are closed. After you leave Scotland, you'll want to come back again—back to this lonely glen and back to the cheerful atmosphere of Kintail Lodge.

Proprietors: Stuart and Margaret Henderson. *Recreational facilities:* Ocean and river swimming, hunting, boat rental at the hotel; sea fishing and boat trips a short drive away. *Facilities for children:* Baby-sitting. *Other facilities:* Lounge, library, cocktail bar, public bar, laundry, garden, playground. *Rooms:* 10, 7 with bath. 2-day minimum advance reservation in season. Off-season rates; reduction for children under 9 sharing. Moderate. *Restaurant service:* Early and late snacks, tea, dinner. *Credit cards:* Master, Visa. *How to get there:* The hotel is on Route A87 at the end of Loch Duich between Kyle of Lochalsh and Fort William. *Telephone:* (059) 981 275.

Gullane, Lothian

GREYWALLS

The ornament of a house is the friends who frequent it.
Ralph Waldo Emerson

The register of exquisite Greywalls reads like *Who's Who*. Edward VII was a guest when it was still a private home, but since the hotel opened in 1948 the guest list has continued to be star-studded. Princess Margaret has come, as have Jack Nicklaus, Lee Trevino, Arnold Palmer, Christopher Lee, Brigitte Bardot, Andy Williams, and Yehudi Menuhin, to name a few. Guests return over and over again.

The house was designed in 1901 by the famous English architect Sir Edwin Lutyens, who said it was his favorite. Gardens were designed by the equally famous Gertrude Jekyll. Some rooms overlook the Muirfield golf course, where the British Open was played in 1980, but even better are those looking out to a walled rose garden. Furniture is original, with a wealth of antiques; extravagant bouquets are everywhere. If King Edward returned to the library he would find everything much as he left it — leatherbound books, a grand piano, Oriental rugs, big down-filled chairs. But the modern bathrooms now fitted into every possible space would be unfamiliar to him; the whole of the splendid mansion originally contained only one.

Greywalls is luxurious but not intimidating. Giles and Ros Weaver set the style for the friendly atmosphere; the staff is smiling, kind, and efficient, and guests feel very much at ease. Some people say that Greywalls serves the best food of any hotel in Britain. Those who love understated elegance will enjoy it here at one of Britain's loveliest country hotels.

Proprietors: Giles and Ros Weaver. *Closed:* December through March. *Recreational facilities:* Tennis at the hotel; outdoor pool, ocean swimming, squash, golf, boat rental, and boat trips a short drive away. *Facilities for children:* Baby-listening. *Other facilities:* Drawing room, TV lounge, library, morning room, sun parlor, cocktail bar, garden. *Rooms:* 22 with bath, TV, and telephone. Ground-floor rooms. Off-season rates; 3-day reduction; discount for children sharing (free if under 3). Very expensive. *Restaurant service:* Luncheon, snacks all day and evening; tea, dinner (coat and tie). *Credit cards:* Amex, Master, Visa. *How to get there:* Take Route A1 south from Edinburgh, then Route A198 toward North Berwick. The hotel is signposted in Gullane, just 40 minutes from central Edinburgh. *Telephone:* (0620) 842 144. *Agent in the United States:* Abercrombie and Kent. [T]

BROWNS' HOTEL

> Hail ye small sweet courtesies of life, for smooth do ye make the road of it.
>
> *Laurence Sterne,* 1768

"A classy place with very good food." That's the way our Scottish niece described Browns' Hotel to us. She was right. This town hotel is an endearing mixture of elegance and coziness within. The house, in a residential area and with lovely gardens, was built in 1810 in Georgian style. Light streams through the glass dome of a cupola over the winding staircase. The house is decorated with strong colors in unusual combinations, put together with flair and good taste. Bedrooms are supremely comfortable, and bathrooms are streamlined.

Antiques combine with thick wall-to-wall carpet, and what isn't antique is very nice. Colin Brown does all the cooking in this appealing hotel he and his mother run so well. The set menu changes daily. It is so well thought of by local residents that you should reserve for your dinner when you engage your room, or the small dining room could be unable to seat you.

The royal burgh of Haddington is a pleasant small town in one of the most prosperous farming areas of Scotland. It's a golfer's paradise with fourteen courses within a twenty-minute drive. John Knox, who founded the Presbyterian Church, was probably born here.

Proprietors: Margaret and Colin Brown. *Closed:* November 1–15. *Recreational facilities:* Indoor pool and squash a short walk away; ocean swimming, tennis, riding, and golf a short drive away. *Other facilities:* Lounge, cocktail lounge, garden. *Rooms:* 6, 4 with bath. Inexpensive. *Restaurant service:* Dinner (by reservation). *How to get there:* Browns' Hotel is on West Road, the main road into Haddington off Route A1 from Edinburgh. *Telephone:* (062 082) 2254. [T]

CULLODEN HOUSE HOTEL

> Culloden, alone of all the battle-fields known to me, is
> still drenched with the melancholy of its association: it is
> the only battle-field I know which contains the graves of
> the fallen, buried in trenches as they died.
> *H.V. Morton,* 1929

This remarkably beautiful Adam-style mansion, built in 1772, stands
within forty acres of parkland beside the battlefield of Culloden. It is said
that Bonnie Prince Charlie spent the night before the battle in the castle
that then occupied this site.

Behind the classical stone facade, lofty rooms with ornate plasterwork
ceilings are furnished with antiques. Candles lend a soft glow to the high-
ceilinged dining room, resplendent with silver, linen, and fresh flowers,
that has an established reputation for good food. Bedrooms, some with
four-posters, are large and well appointed, most with views over the
surrounding hills. Bathrooms are modern, some even sporting Jacuzzi
baths.

We've learned much Scottish history during our visits to the Visitor
Centre and Museum of Culloden, which has an audiovisual exhibit. The
moor itself is at once romantic and tragic, haunted by the memory of the
terrible battle that crushed Gaelic Scotland's hopes forever. Simple
headstones over mass graves bear individual clan names.

Proprietors: Ian and Marjory McKenzie. *Recreational facilities:*
Tennis, sauna, and solarium at the hotel. Riding nearby. Fishing,
shooting, and deer-stalking arranged. *Other facilities:* Lounge, library,
cocktail bar, garden. *Rooms:* 20 with bath, telephone, and TV. *Restau-
rant service:* Luncheon snacks, tea, dinner. *Credit cards:* Amex, Diners,
Visa. *How to get there:* The hotel is 3 miles northeast of Inverness on
Route A96. *Telephone:* (0463) 790461. *Agent in the United States:* Scott
Calder. [T]

Kincraig, Highland

OSSIAN

Oh for the crags that are wild and majestic!
Lord Byron

The Ossian is easy to reach but seems isolated. A cheerful guest house where true Scottish hospitality marks the friendly service, it's a solid stone building furnished with many antiques and warm wall-to-wall carpets. Bedrooms are all different; one has an oak suite with an elaborate ceiling-high headboard. Others command a view of the granite domes of the Cairngorms, as do the bay windows of the living room and the rustic seating in the garden. A family chef prepares à la carte meals, with wine if you wish, served in an adjoining building. There is also a tea and craft shop where you can stop for morning coffee or afternoon tea. Scones and cakes are home baked.

For anyone interested in trying a new sport, this area has it all. Besides skiing, there are courses in salmon and trout fishing, a canoeing and sailing school, beginners' lessons in rock climbing, horseback riding, gliding, even the Scottish game of curling. You can rent ice skates or ski all summer on a snowless practice slope.

At the Clan Tartan Centre at Aviemore, a computer will take only seconds to research your name if it's Scottish, or if you wonder if it might be. You'll learn of any clan connection: about its chief, heraldic crest, tartan, origins, and war cry. Then you can buy some of your tartan right there. A historical exhibit and a continuous show relate the history of the plaids. There is also a new Whisky Tasting Museum where nearly all the Scotches can be sampled.

If you check the rates at the Ossian, you'll see that it gives very good value. You'll find it a happy haven, the sort of place where you'll make new friends.

Proprietors: Lynn and John Rainbow and Marion and John Ramage. *Closed:* November and January. *Recreational facilities:* Lake and river swimming, game fishing, boat rental, wind surfing and boat trips a short walk away; indoor pool, tennis, squash, skiing, riding, ice-skating, and golf a short drive away. *Other facilities:* Lounge, TV lounge, garden. *Rooms:* 11 sharing baths. 1-week minimum advance reservation in August. Discount for children under 13. Inexpensive. *Restaurant service:* Snacks, tea, supper, dinner. *Credit cards:* Master, Visa. *How to get there:* The Ossian is signposted in the village of Kincraig, which is off the Scenic Route between Aviemore and Kingussie. Guests can be met at a railway station in Aviemore or Kingussie. *Telephone:* (05404) 242.

Kingussie, Highland

OSPREY HOTEL

> In Heav'n itself I'll ask no more
> Than just a Highland welcome.
>
> *Robert Burns*

For those who enjoy informal country inns but like also a hint of sophistication, the Osprey Hotel is the perfect answer and a place we'd recommend for more than overnight.

For a stay of several days, we usually prefer an inn in a village where we can get out and walk about, absorbing local life. As Kingussie is one of the most central villages in Scotland, we can't think of any place we'd prefer to stop for a week than at this hotel.

It is decorated with flair and many antiques, and the home cooking is outstanding. Prime Scottish beef, lamb, free-range chickens, are stars of the menu, and justly so. For fish lovers there are salmon and trout from local rivers, quite outstanding whether fresh or peat-smoked. All desserts are baked right in the kitchen. Breakfast specialties include Scottish oatmeal porridge, oak-smoked haddocks and kippers, local heather honey, as well as fresh eggs, bacon, and freshly ground coffee. Few small establishments have a cellar like the one at the Osprey. It features more than 120 wines, ranging from excellent inexpensive house wines to superb clarets dating back to 1959, all at good value. To keep you cozy, you'll find wall-to-wall carpets, electric blankets, and heated towel bars.

At nearby Loch Garten Nature Reserve, ospreys, extinct in Scotland for many years, returned to breed in 1959. Their treetop eyrie may be viewed through fixed binoculars from the Observation Hut.

As you can walk to the Osprey from the train station, this is an ideal stop for train travelers.

Proprietors: Duncan and Pauline Reeves. *Closed:* November and December. *Recreational facilities:* River swimming, tennis, golf, and salmon and trout fishing a walk away. *Facilities for children:* Baby-listening. *Other facilities:* Lounge, TV lounge. *Rooms:* 9, 2 with bath. Off-season rate; reduction for children. Inexpensive. *Restaurant service:* Tea, dinner. *Credit cards:* Amex, Diners, Master, Visa. *How to get there:* The hotel is just off Route A9 in Kingussie village. The railway station is a short walk from the hotel. *Telephone:* (05402) 510.

Ledaig, Strathclyde

ISLE OF ERISKA

> My heart's in the Highlands, my heart is not here,
> My heart's in the Highlands a-chasing the deer.
>
> *Robert Burns*

The Isle of Eriska has so much to recommend it that it's hard to know where to start. Most important, perhaps, is the house-party atmosphere of great warmth and friendliness that initiates with the owners, Robin and Sheena Buchanan-Smith. They are around each evening before dinner chatting with guests and introducing them to each other.

The hotel, a turreted, towered, and bay-windowed Victorian baronial mansion, is set romantically on its own 300-acre island in the Firth of Lorn. Wildlife abounds to give the place the air of a natural sanctuary; roe deer, badgers, herons, and even an occasional golden eagle can be observed. Rhododendron, azaleas, daffodils and bluebells add their beauty. Much of the hotel's food served is right from the estate – milk and cream from a Jersey herd, eggs from free-range hens, vegetables and berries from the garden, and beef from shaggy Highland cattle that graze on hill and moor. Sheena, a Cordon Bleu cook, sets high standards for the kitchen. Breakfast is hearty: bacon, eggs, kidneys, and porridge buffet-style under silver domes; quantities of good coffee and tea; hot toast and homebaked brown bread with homemade marmalades. All guests book for the set dinner (coat and tie, please) that might start with smoked haddock mousse, continue with soup followed by roast beef and garden vegetables and a selection of desserts (try the fruit tarts with heavy cream), and finish off with a grand cheese board. The wine list is very well chosen. Morning coffee and afternoon tea are served to house guests in the lounge at no charge.

Public rooms are full of character – beautiful Oriental rugs, wood-paneled walls, floral chintz, brown leather, huge piles of logs beside open hearths, books, magazines. Some bedrooms have antiques, most have modern furniture, but all have good reading lights, fruit, flowers, sewing kits, and modern bathrooms with heated towel-bars. Single rooms are just half the price of the doubles.

Robin, who is a yachtsman (and also a minister), can make arrangements for guests to charter a 7-ton Bermudian-rigged sailing yacht with skipper. Less expensive boat trips are available nearby.

Proprietors: Robin and Sheena Buchanan-Smith. *Closed:* November through February. *Recreational facilities:* Tennis, loch swimming (very cold), and riding at the hotel; golf and boat trips a short drive away. *Facilities for children:* Baby-listening, children's supper, pony. *Other facilities:* Drawing room, lounge, library, cocktail bar, garden. *Rooms:* 21 with bath and telephone. Suitable for wheelchair guests. 4-day reduction; discount for children sharing. Very expensive. *Restaurant service:* Luncheon, dinner by reservation. *Credit card:* Amex, Master. *How to get there:* Isle of Eriska is signposted on Route A828 north of Ledaig, which is between Ballachulish and Connell. Guests can be met at the Connell railway station or airport. *Telephone:* (0631 72) 371. *Agent in the United States:* David Mitchell. [T]

Lockerbie, Dumfries and Galloway

DRYFESDALE HOTEL

> All my life long I had longed to see heather
> In the land of my kinsmen far over the sea.
>> *Marguerite Wilkinson,* 1920

The Dryfesdale Hotel offers a warm welcome to those entering Scotland. An eighteenth-century former manse, its window-walled sun-room, added forty years ago, commands a panoramic view of the rolling farmland of the Border country.

Log fires enhance an appealing lounge furnished with traditional and antique pieces. There are hunting prints and stags' heads in the attractive bar. Good food is served in the dining room, and a gracious winding stairway leads to bedrooms that are on the small side.

Although it is within sight of a main road that links Scotland and England, the Dryfesdale Hotel stands quiet and peaceful on 7 acres. Its convenient location makes it a fine place for a first night's stay in the land of the heather.

Proprietors: James and Jean Bell. *Closed:* One week for New Year's. *Recreational facilities:* Riding at the hotel; golf, tennis, salmon and sea-trout fishing, and hunting nearby. *Other facilities:* Lounge, sun lounge, cocktail bar, garden. *Rooms:* 10, 8 with bath, all with telephone and TV; 1 self-catering cottage; some rooms suitable for wheelchair guests. 3-day reduction; off-season rates November through March; discount for children under 14 sharing. Inexpensive to moderate. *Restaurant service:* Luncheon, snacks, tea, dinner. *Credit cards:* Amex, Diners, Master, Visa. *How to get there:* From the south on A74, take the third sign marked Lockerbie and find hotel signposted. From the north, take the first sign marked Lockerbie and cross over the highway. *Telephone:* (057 62) 2427.

Nairn, Highland

CLIFTON HOTEL

I am one of those who always think it fun to be in Scotland.

Hilaire Belloc, 1942

This romantic hotel of unusual character seems to be a country house but is within walking distance of everything in town. "Theatrical" is a word often used to describe its style. The rooms are warmed by vivacious colors, as well as by log fires. Hand-blocked wallpaper sets off fine Victorian antiques and chintz- and velvet-covered furniture; the walls are embellished with paintings and gilt-framed mirrors. Service and comfort get high marks. J. Gordon Macintyre is responsible for this long-established hotel's present exuberant charm. He enjoys telling stories of its Victorian past.

In the dining room main courses include some unusual ones but also standard roasts for the less adventurous. You'll serve yourself from a memorable dessert buffet.

Beds are made up with Continental quilts, but if you prefer sheets and blankets, as we do, ask for them when you reserve your room. The old custom of bringing an early-morning cup of tea to your bedroom is still followed here, and a full breakfast may be eaten in your bedroom or in the dining room, which faces the sea. If you are passing through Nairn, this is a good spot for lunch or afternoon tea.

No visitor to Scotland should miss nearby Culloden, now a peaceful tract of moorland, where the exhausted Jacobites under Bonnie Prince Charlie suffered a terrible slaughter at the hands of the red-coated army of the English Hanoverian king in 1746. An audio-visual presentation at the Visitor's Centre tells of the battle and the history of Scotland.

Proprietor: J. Gordon Macintyre. *Closed:* November through February. *Recreational facilities:* Ocean swimming at the hotel; indoor pool, tennis, and squash nearby. *Other facilities:* Drawing room, writing room, TV room, cocktail bar, garden. *Rooms:* 17 with bath. Moderate. *Restaurant service:* Luncheon, snacks, tea, dinner (coat and tie required). *Credit card:* Amex. *How to get there:* Nairn is on Route A96 east of Inverness. Take Marine Road toward the ocean. Turn left on Seafield Street. The hotel will be on your left. Guests arriving by train in Nairn may telephone the hotel to be picked up. Guests can be met at the Inverness airport. *Telephone:* (0667) 53119.

ROSEDALE HOTEL

From the lone shieling of the misty island
Mountains divide us, and the waste of seas—
Yet still the blood is strong, the heart is Highland
And we in dreams behold the Hebrides.

John Galt

The Rosedale Hotel is directly on the waterfront in the heart of Portree, the capital of Skye, largest island of the Inner Hebrides. It consists of several whitewashed, early-nineteenth-century buildings that were built against a sharp slope. Entrance is at the top level from the street side that faces the village center and at the bottom level from the quay along the harbor. Erratic stairways go up and down every which way. Furnishings are plain modern, but the atmosphere of the hotel, decorated with pretty colors, is light and airy, very pleasant and friendly. The dining room faces the water on the middle level. Ask for a bedroom that has the same harbor view.

If you are using a BritRail pass, you may think you cannot reach Portree, but a bus that will take you to the Rosedale Hotel meets the ferry that crosses to Skye frequently from Kyle of Lochalsh on the mainland. The 30-mile drive from ferry to hotel brings into view brooding mountains that rise straight from the sea, but Portree itself is a lively little town visited by steamers and fishing boats of all kinds. When you return to the mainland, you will carry with you happy memories of your visit to the fabled Isle of the Mist.

Proprietor: Hugh Andrew. *Closed:* October through April. *Recreational facilities:* Boat trips from the hotel; indoor pool, tennis, and squash a short walk away. *Other facilities:* Lounge, TV lounge, cocktail bar, public bar. *Rooms:* 21, 16 with bath. Off-season rates. Inexpensive. *Restaurant service:* Snacks, tea, dinner. *How to get there:* Take the ferry to the Isle of Skye from either Mallaig or Kyle of Lochalsh. Take Route A850 north to Portree. Or take the train to Kyle of Lochalsh, ferry to Kyleakin, then bus to Portree. *Telephone:* (0478) 2531.   [T]

St Andrews, Fife

RUFFLETS HOTEL

> In the fields called the Links, the citizens . . . divert
> themselves at a game called golf . . . they use a curious
> kind of bats tipped with horn, and small balls of leather,
> stuffed with feathers. . . . This they strike with such
> force . . . from one hole to another, that they will fly to
> an incredible distance.
>
> *Tobias Smollett,* 1771

The historic university city St Andrews is known to golfers all over the
world as the home of the Royal and Ancient Golf Club. Mary, Queen of

Scots, played golf, as did Charles I and James II. In 1834 William IV approved the title "Royal and Ancient" for the course at St Andrews. Visitors may play the game on its hallowed turf.

Rufflets Hotel, on the outskirts of the city, is delightful. To the once private mansion was added a large cocktail bar, where we enjoyed talking first to students from St Andrews University, then to a group of men from all over Britain who meet here once each year to golf together. Walls are decorated with a collection of prints by Sir William Russel Flint.

Vegetables from the hotel's garden are served at candlelit dinners in a dining room overlooking lawns with a nine-hole putting green. A small stream wanders across the back of the large garden, crossed by little bridges along the garden paths, and an extensive flower garden supplies bright bouquets daily.

You should apply two months ahead for a starting time at the Old Course. Write for information about advance reservations to the hotel. We were able to play without having made a reservation by giving our names to the hotel desk before 2 P.M. The hotel calls the starter, and at 3 P.M. names are drawn for cancellations for the next day's starting times. If you don't win one of these, ask the hotel to arrange for you to play on one of the other three courses: Jubilee, Eden, and New. They are open Sundays, but the Old Course is not.

For nongolfers there are sandy beaches and good shops. A visit to the St Andrew Woolen Mills, beside the Old Course, is a must.

Proprietor: Mrs. Russell. *Closed:* January. *Recreational facilities:* 9-hole putting green at the hotel; indoor pool, ocean swimming, tennis, sauna, riding, golf, and freshwater fishing a short drive away. *Facilities for children:* Baby-listening. *Other facilities:* 2 lounges, TV lounge, cocktail bar, garden. *Rooms:* 21 with bath and telephone. Suitable for wheelchair guests. 3-day reduction; 2-day breaks; free for children under 10 sharing; Christmas and New Year's programs. Moderate. *Restaurant service:* Luncheon, snacks, supper, dinner. *Credit cards:* Amex, Diners, Master, Visa. How to get there: The hotel is on Strathkinness Low Road, Route B939. *Telephone:* (0334) 72594. [T]

Selkirk, Borders

PHILIPBURN HOUSE HOTEL

> A mist of memory broods and floats,
> The Border waters flow;
> The air is full of ballad notes,
> Borne out of long ago.
>
> *Andrew Lang,* 1899

Philipburn House is one of the friendliest hotels in Scotland, and a must for anyone traveling with children. Normally those without children do not seek out family hotels, but they shouldn't avoid this one. Supervised hiking and horseback riding, playgrounds, game rooms, and early suppers take care of young guests so well that the rest of us can enjoy both socializing in lounge or bar and gourmet dining without noisy interruption.

Jim Hill, architect turned innkeeper, skillfully modified and added to an eighteenth-century house set in 4 acres of garden. The inn is now an attractive and unusual mix of modern furnishings, antiques, wicker, and bamboo. Some new bedrooms with pine ceilings have sliding glass doors that lead to private terraces overlooking a swimming pool. There are several family suites with bunkrooms for the children.

Jim is also a dedicated chef and supervises cooking that is worth remembering. The menu might include casserole of game with oranges, grouse wrapped in bacon, Dover sole simmered in butter and vermouth, and salmon and trout from the nearby Ettrick and Yarrow rivers. For dessert, such delights as fresh peach cake laced with peach brandy, Westmorland nut-and-raisin flan, or Grand Marnier soufflé make choosing difficult. Wines are Jim's hobby; an extraordinary cellar offers nearly three hundred — some dating back to 1929.

A jovial personality about the hotel is David Fordyce, who leads guests on rambles into the hills, tends bar wearing his kilt, and recites native poetry in Scots dialect. He enjoys sharing with guests his extensive knowledge of the history and legends of the Border. Sir Walter Scott's home, Abbotsford, is just 4 miles away, and the great abbeys of Dryburgh, Jedburgh, and Melrose are all within a very short drive. Even nonshoppers will want to go to the nearby woolen mill that offers bargains in Scottish tweeds.

If you can't stay, stop for lunch or for afternoon tea, which is served by the pool or under garden trees when the weather is warm enough. This distinctive hotel is just over the border from England and the place for those who have time for only a dip into Scotland. Because of its friendliness and outstanding food, it is one of our favorites. We'd like to go back and stay a week.

Proprietors: Jim and Anne Hill. *Closed:* January. *Recreational facilities:* Outdoor pool and badminton at the hotel; indoor pool a short walk away; tennis, riding, hunting, golf, shooting, and salmon and trout fishing a short drive away. *Facilities for children:* Baby-sitting and -listening; children's playground. *Other facilities:* Lounge, TV lounge, 2 cocktail bars, games room, garden. *Rooms:* 16, 12 with bath, all with TV and tea-making. Suitable for wheelchair guests. 4-day reduction; 2-day breaks; reduction for children sharing. Moderate. *Restaurant service:* Luncheon, snacks, tea, dinner. *Credit cards:* Amex, Diners, Visa. *How to get there:* Leave Selkirk going west on Route A706. The hotel is on the right. *Telephone:* (0750) 20747.

WALES

LLWYNDERW

In Wales there are jewels
To gather, but with the eye
Only.

R.S. Thomas, 1913

Llwynderw is a jewel, the only luxury hotel in the wild highlands of central Wales. Away from it all for sure, it is perched at 1,000 feet without another building in sight. More than 80 species of birds have been seen in or close to the garden, where azaleas and rhododendron bloom profusely. Ancient beeches and oaks protect the house, a stone mansion dating from 1796.

Beautiful furnishings include antiques, Oriental rugs, velvet and brocade upholstery, crystal chandeliers, chintz draperies, paintings, and books—lots of lovely books. Fires blaze in the dining room, drawing room, and library. Some bedrooms have lace bedspreads and others Welsh tapestry. One has two wing chairs, and those on the third floor have high beamed ceilings. Attractive presentation is a feature of the cuisine, a combination of French and traditional English cooking. A set dinner is without choices except for desserts. Bread is homemade, and water comes from a spring on the property.

Tapes can be hired from the hotel that give historical and cultural information for excursions in all directions. Llwynderw (for pronunciation you're on your own) is very personally run by Michael Yates, who has no television in the house to disturb the peace. You'll meet him and the staff as well as the other guests; it's that sort of place.

Proprietor: Michael Yates. *Closed:* Late October to Easter. *Recreational facilities:* Riding nearby. *Other facilities:* Sitting room, library, conservatory, garden. *Rooms:* 10 with bath. 2-night reduction. No children under 10. Expensive to very expensive. *Restaurant service:* Luncheon and dinner by reservation. *Credit card:* Amex. *How to get there:* From Llanwrtyd Wells, take the road to Abergwesyn. Llynderw is signposted on the left. *Telephone:* (05913) 238. *Agent in the United States:* Abercrombie and Kent.   [T]

Bontddu, Gwynedd

BONTDDU HALL

> You look inland where the salt tide swirls and eddies,
> towards the mountains round Dolgelley. They lie folded
> against one another in long gentle line, flaming with
> gorse, green with grass, the darker belts of woodland
> climbing in the hollows.
>
> *H. V. Morton*

This jewel of a hotel, surely one of the finest in Wales, is a fresh, blithe
place, an endearing mixture of elegance and informality. It began life as
an imposing Victorian baronial pile set on a height. Its decor, encompass-
ing a surprising range of styles, is exceptional. Some rooms are grand,
with heavy, carved antiques. A lounge, in great contrast, has white
bamboo furniture covered with pastel pinks, greens, and yellows, surprising and effective under a wood-beamed ceiling. A window wall of the
dining room, which has won high recommendations, gives views over the
Mawddach estuary and Cader Idris range of mountains, the scene described by H. V. Morton above.

Several acres of cultivated gardens are enhanced by stone walls and
statuary. Visitors come for the food and luxury, but perhaps the main
attraction is the warm hospitality. Bill Hall, a true hotelier, has owned
Bontddu Hall (pronounced Bonthee) for over forty years and has files
full of unsolicited letters of praise from former guests.

Many hotels boast that each bedroom is different, but here the variations are enormous. Some have draped beds and lush colors; one has brass beds and summery green and white matching wallpaper and curtains; each stylish modern lodge room in a new addition on an elevated site has a magnificent view from a private sun balcony. When we think of Bontddu Hall, we see the lovely rooms, the magnificent trees, the dramatic views, and we wish we were there.

Proprietor: Bill Hall. *Closed:* Mid-October to Easter. *Recreational facilities:* Ocean swimming, riding, boat rental (canoe, row, sail, motor), boat trips, and deep-sea fishing a short drive away. *Other facilities:* Drawing room, lounge, sun parlor, cocktail bar, public bar, garden. *Rooms:* 24 with bath, TV, and telephone. Ground-floor rooms. Off-season rates (almost 50% less); breaks. No children under 3; children under 16 free if sharing. Moderate. *Restaurant service:* Luncheon, snacks, tea, dinner. *Credit cards:* Amex, Carte Blanche, Diners, Master, Visa. *How to get there:* The hotel is on Route A496 between Barmouth and Dolgellau. *Telephone:* (034 149) 661.   [T]

GLIFFAES COUNTRY HOUSE

> I care not, I, to fish in seas
> Fresh river best my mind do please.
>
> *William Basse,* 1653

On the terrace we basked in the spring sun. Lawns rolled rather steeply away to where the River Usk gleamed silver far below, an angler on its banks casting for salmon. Across the river, cattle grazed placidly on verdant meadows. This is a place to relax, surrounded by nature's beauty. Fishing is a main attraction. The hotel owns more than 2 miles of the Usk, reputed to be one of the best salmon and trout rivers in the British Isles.

A long driveway flanked by showy rhododendrons leads to the im-

posing house, built as a private mansion in 1885. One of its two distinctive towers holds a chiming clock, silent during the night. Twenty-seven acres of parkland and gardens contain some of the rarest and most beautiful trees in Wales. Despite its outward magnificence, the Gliffaes is not a luxury hotel, but it is comfortable and pleasant. Mr. and Mrs. Brabner, resident owners, encourage friendliness.

Afternoon tea is set out buffet style; the country-style food served at this hotel includes vegetables grown in the garden. Our bedroom was large, with a balcony that had the same lovely view we enjoyed from the terrace.

This hotel is set in a national park in gentle mountains called the Brecon Beacons, unspoiled countryside ideal for the bird-watcher. Pony-trekking through its hills and valleys can be arranged. On Llangorse Lake, 8 miles away, sailing and water-skiing are available.

Proprietors: Mr. and Mrs. Nick Brabner. *Closed:* January 1—March 15. *Recreational facilities:* Tennis with a pro available, river swimming, salmon and trout fishing, and nine-hole putting green at the hotel; riding, boating, and water-skiing a short drive away. *Other facilities:* Drawing room, lounge, cocktail bar, billiard room, garden. *Rooms:* 19 with bath and tea-making. Reduction; 2-day breaks. Inexpensive to moderate. *Restaurant service:* Luncheon, snacks, tea, dinner. *Credit cards:* Amex, Master, Visa. *How to get there:* Take Route A40 west from Abergavenny to about 2½ miles beyond Crickhowell. Turn left and follow signs to Gliffaes House, 1 mile farther on. *Telephone:* (0874) 730371.

RHYD GARN WEN

My garden is a pleasant place
Of sun glory and leaf grace,
O Friend, wherever you may be
Will you not come to visit me?

Louise Driscoll, 1927

The garden at Rhyd Garn Wen is not the only thing about it that is pleasant. The house, the food, and the owners are all delightful. Huw Jones wanted a change of pace from his life as a TV producer for the BBC and found it here in remote western Wales. He was cutting a swath of lawn when he greeted us from the seat of his power mower. Susan, who went to culinary school for a year before opening the restaurant, has won accolades in all British food guides for her exceptional cooking at reasonable prices.

There is a small choice on a menu that changes every evening. Your dinner might start with an asparagus or French onion tart, a cheese soufflé, or homemade soup, and move on to guinea fowl stuffed with apples served with Calvados sauce or fillets of sole rolled around a mousseline of trout with a prawn sauce. As the house is just over a mile from the sea, all fish is fresh. Local veal and duck are favorites. Dessert might be lemon pudding, fresh fruits with cream, or an all-Welsh cheeseboard. The wine list is professional, Huw being a connoisseur.

Guests enjoy coffee and petit fours in the living room while chatting together before a fire. No proprietors could be more relaxed and hospitable. Their serene Victorian house is furnished with antiques and comfortable seating and offers only three bedrooms. Book ahead, as the word is out about this lovely place.

Proprietors: Huw and Susan Jones. *Closed:* November to Easter. *Recreational facilities:* Ocean swimming, surfing, windsurfing, row- and sailboat rental, trout, salmon, and deep-sea fishing, tennis, golf, riding, and indoor pool nearby. *Other facilities:* Living room, TV room, cocktail bar, garden. *Rooms:* 3 with bath. Moderate. *Restaurant service:* Dinner by reservation. *Credit card:* Master. *How to get there:* From Route A487, 3 miles south of Cardigan, turn east on the only crossroad in the village of Croft. Rhyd Garn Wen is on the right. *Telephone:* (0239) 612742.

GLANRANNELL PARK HOTEL

These are the things I prize
And hold of dearest worth;
Light of the sapphire skies,
Peace of the silent hills,
Shelter of forests, comforts of the grass,
Music of birds, murmur of little rills,
And after showers,
The smell of flowers,
And of the good brown earth,
And best of all, along the way,
Friendship and mirth.   *Henry Van Dyke,* 1892

The things prized by Henry Van Dyke, in his little poem above, he would find at this peaceful, friendly hotel today. Bronwyn and David Davies owned a small London hotel before they returned to Wales some years ago to open this country house. Would that all hotels could boast such agreeable and obliging proprietors.

The house is surrounded by lawns and overlooks a lake. Books are distributed among the pleasant, comfy rooms that are plainly decorated, with linen antimacassars protecting floral upholstery. Good country cooking that includes homemade bread uses local produce whenever possible. Afternoon tea is a specialty, with Welsh cakes and scones. Picnic lunches are provided when desired. The wine cellar boasts a good selection.

David raises Welsh cobs on his 23 acres. Glanrannell Park bears a plaque for being the house that raised the prize pony Dyowl Starlight in about 1900, the Welsh stud from which all registered Welsh cobs are descended. A flock of black Welsh mountain sheep share the paddocks. David, who speaks fluent Welsh, makes Welsh musical instruments.

Proprietors: Bronwyn and David Davies. *Recreational facilities:* Salmon and sea-trout fishing and riding nearby. *Facilities for children:* Baby-sitting. *Other facilities:* Sitting room, TV room, cocktail bar, garden. *Rooms:* 8, 5 with bath. Reduction for children sharing (free under 2). Inexpensive. *Restaurant service:* Snacks, tea, dinner. *How to get there:* The hotel is on Route 4302 just south of Route 482, between Llanwrda and Lampeter. *Telephone:* (05583) 230.

Glyn Ceiriog, Clwyd

GOLDEN PHEASANT

Oh, the wild hills of Wales, the land of old renown and of wonder.

George Borrow

This unusual country inn is renowned for the excellence of the sports it offers. Imagine yourself riding through heather, purple against a blue sky. Experienced riders go off in small groups, beginners are given lessons by expert instructors. The Turners raise registered Welsh cobs.

Shooting? All kinds are catered to, from covert shooting to grouse driving, and for partridge, pheasant, or mallards in season. Fishing? Catch salmon on a privately owned beat of the Welsh Dee and on the Severn; sea trout and brown trout on the Ceiriog; rainbow and brown trout on Lake Vyrnwy, an hour away through magnificent country. Anyone serious about these sports should write well in advance, get the brochures, and make arrangements.

The hotel conducts guided walks, not too arduous so all can take part, that meander over fields and moors, along lanes and over the hills. A convivial atmosphere prevails throughout. Some walks start from the hotel; for others, the walkers climb into a Safari Land-Rover to drive to scenic areas before commencing the walk.

Part of this congenial inn dates back to 1755, when it was a brewery. Mrs. Turner is acclaimed for her cooking, which features sirloin of beef, Welsh lamb, game in season, "roasted, casseroled, and in crusty pies." Guests come for the homemade soups and Dee salmon. Desserts are homebaked, from apple pie to luscious cakes. Under the 1775 beams in the bar, a fire in a grate sets off burnished horse brasses, and walls are hung with fox heads, guns, and sporting prints.

Each season brings its own delights: in spring, apple trees blossom, Welsh lambs and Welsh foals frolic; in summer, daylight lasts until after ten, for sitting in the garden; in autumn, crisp days sparkle and leaves turn to many hues; in winter, the hunt meets and hearty winter teas are enjoyed by the fire. This inn is a marvelous stop for a single traveler. There are two single rooms that rent for just half the double rate, and it's easy to meet the other guests.

Proprietors: The Turner family. *Recreational facilities:* Riding, hunting, fishing, shooting, and guided walks from the hotel. *Facilities for children:* Free supper for children under 12; riding lessons. *Other facilities:* Lounge, TV lounge, cocktail bar, public bar, garden. *Rooms:* 19 with bath, TV, telephone, and tea-making. 2-day reduction; breaks; discount for children; Christmas program; New Year's program. Moderate. *Restaurant service:* Luncheon, snacks, dinner. *Credit cards:* Amex, Master. *How to get there:* Take Route A5 to Chirk, then Route B4500 through Glyn Ceiriog to Llwynmawr. Guests can be met at the Chirk railway station. *Telephone:* (069 172) 281. *Agent in the United States:* Josephine Barr. [T]

LAKE VYRNWY HOTEL

> For when one hill behind your back you see
> Another comes, two times as high as he!
> *Thomas Churchyard,* 1587

Set high on a rugged Welsh hill, the Lake Vyrnwy Hotel offers solid British comfort. It's brochure states: "We try to run the hotel as much like a private house as we can. It aims at being a comfortable, old-fashioned sporting hotel and makes no concession to any modern image. The food is of the traditional country-house type, with the best possible ingredients used."

The hotel has a turn-of-the-century quality—reminiscent of the days when families of substance came yearly to settle in for weeks at a time. Log fires in large lounges add to the warm hospitable atmosphere. You'll be lucky if you can get one of the traditionally furnished bedrooms with sweeping views over Lake Vyrnwy.

Meals are among the highlights of a stay here, featuring generous helpings of British cooking at its best. Roasts and game, homemade soups and desserts are always on the dinner menu. Luncheon is chosen from an extensive buffet, except on Sunday when the traditional roast beef dinner stars.

The hotel holds fishing rights to all of Lake Vyrnwy, stocked with brown and rainbow trout, and holds shooting rights over vast moors. Reservations for shooting must be made months in advance.

By some quirk in the postal system, mail is addressed by way of England, but the hotel is many miles west of the English border. This is a good center for exploring the enchanting countryside of north-central Wales and the magnificent Snowdonia National Park.

Proprietors: Mrs. J.F. Moir and Lt. Col. Sir John Baynes. *Closed:* Mid-January through February. *Recreational facilities:* Fishing and tennis at the hotel. *Other facilities:* Lounge, TV lounge, cocktail bar, billiard room, laundry service, and garden. *Facilities for children:* Children's supper; games room. *Rooms:* 31, 11 with bath. Reduction for children. Elevator. Inexpensive to moderate. *Restaurant service:* Luncheon, tea, dinner (coat and tie, please). *Mailing addresss:* Llanwddyn, via Oswestry, Shropshire, SY10 0LY. *How to get there:* The hotel is on the southern tip of Lake Vyrnwy, signposted on B4396. *Telephone:* (069 173) 244.

Llanarmon D.C., Clwyd

THE WEST ARMS

Everything the landscape painter could want was to be found in North Wales.

Richard Wilson, 1775

In this land of song and rugged hills, there is a remote valley, little known to Americans, where you will find an inn of the picture-book kind. Much of its charm derives from simple country things—the River Ceiriog tumbling through the village, the rolling, heather-covered hills, the gamboling of new lambs in the spring, the bleating of sheep the only sound to enliven the solitude.

The inn specializes in serving such good Welsh food as spring lamb, fresh salmon, pheasant and other game in season, and home-cooked desserts, with a choice of wines from an extensive list. Pretty posies ornament the tables. Handhewn beams give character to the rooms, where brass and polished mahogany reflect the flames from the cavernous fireplaces. The pub, furnished with oak, including a carved confessional, has been honored as a Pub of the Year for Wales.

Proprietors: Arnold and Jean Edge. *Recreational facilities:* Tennis and fishing at the hotel; golf and riding nearby. *Other facilities:* Lounge, TV lounge, cocktail bar, public bar, garden. *Rooms:* 16, 7 with bath. Suitable for wheelchair guests. Breaks. Inexpensive. *Restaurant service:* Luncheon, snacks, tea, dinner. *Credit card:* Amex, Diners, Master, Visa. *How to get there:* Take Route A5 to Chirk, turn at the church onto Route B4500 for Glyn Ceiriog, and continue to Llanarmon D.C. *Telephone:* (069 176) 665.

GEORGE III HOTEL

Then come who pine for peace and pleasure,
Away from counter, court and school,
Spend here your measure of time and treasure,
And taste the treats of Penmaenpool.
Gerard Manley Hopkins

Right on the water there's a charming little inn that was once a ship chandlery. Sailing ships from here brought slate to the United States and returned with hardwoods to build more ships. Stone benches beside the estuary make a great place to eat lunch while you watch rowboats bobbing at moorings. In the bar you'll find a large selection of snacks—homemade steak and kidney pie, toasted sandwiches, pizzas, and an assortment of salads from a buffet. The dining room, known for good food, specializes in local duck, pheasant, lobster, sea trout, and salmon.

The poet Gerard Manley Hopkins is said to have written the verse above in the guest book when he stayed at the hotel. Its brochure reads, "Our aim is to provide an informal atmosphere coupled with good food and wine, so that you may rejoin the hurly burly of life refreshed." This wonderfully cozy inn succeeds admirably. A cavernous fireplace with an enormous inglenook gives great character to an Old World lounge. The bars hold a wealth of brass and old blue and white china. Traditional bedrooms in delightful strong colors are well furnished. Those in a Victorian building next to the inn are larger, with excellent modern baths.

Proprietor: Gail Hall. *Closed:* Christmas. *Recreational facilities:* Ocean swimming, riding, boat trips, and deep-sea fishing a short drive away. *Facilities for children:* Baby-listening. *Other facilities:* Lounge, cocktail bar, public bar. *Rooms:* 12, 7 with bath, all with TV. 3-day reduction; 2-day breaks; discount for children under 11 sharing. Inexpensive to moderate. *Restaurant service:* Early and late snacks, dinner. *Credit cards:* Amex, Carte Blanche, Diners, Master, Visa. *How to get there:* Penmaenpool is west of Dolgellau on Route A493, at the bridge that crosses the Mawddach estuary. *Telephone:* (0341) 422 525. [T]

Penmorfa, Gwynedd

BWLCH-Y-FEDWEN

> There was no such place, and there never had been any such place, as the hostelry of the coaching age for creature comforts and good service.
>
> *Charles Harper,* 1906

The friendly Bridges will make you feel welcome right away in this snug guest house, once a coaching inn dating back to 1664. The lounge is really a parlor with Victorian and Edwardian furniture and much bric-a-brac on tables, some with tops of needlepoint under glass. Bookcases with interesting books about Wales line one wall, and others display pictures in heavy Victorian frames, Coalport plates, and Royal Crown Derby ornaments. It's a congenial setting where guests talk to each other around a coal fire in the grate. Two golden retrievers not allowed into the parlor were so polite they stood and talked to us from a doorway, tails slowly waving.

The old coaching inn atmosphere is strong in the candlelit dining room, which has stone walls, low beams, and a large hearth. We were very happy with the duckling with stuffing and applesauce, but there was also roast beef with Yorkshire pudding and horseradish sauce. Don't skip dessert—brandy gateau, cherry cream shortcake, hazel meringue.

Plan to visit Caernarvon Castle not far away. We do not tour every castle; we would rather stay in those converted to hotels than take guided tours, but at Caernarvon Castle a guided tour isn't required. We wandered through the vast stone ruin, trying to imagine life here in the Middle Ages. We twisted up tight, spiral stone stairs that sometimes ended abruptly, picked our way through dim passages to turn a corner and find no roof, peered out through slits through which longbowmen once showered arrows to repulse the enemy, saw the room where the present Prince Charles was invested as Prince of Wales, and heard the melodious voices of chattering groups of Welsh schoolchildren. It's a fascinating memory.

Proprietors: Gwyneth and Arthur Bridge. *Closed:* November through March. *Recreational facilities:* Ocean swimming a short drive away. *Other facilities:* Drawing room, TV lounge, sun parlor, cocktail bar, garden. *Rooms:* 6 with bath. 3-day reduction. No children under 12. Inexpensive. *How to get there:* The lodging is on Route A487, the Porthmadog-Caernarvon road. *Telephone:* (0766) 2975.

Talsarnau, Gwynedd

MAES-Y-NEUADD HOTEL

> A morsel of genuine history is a thing so rare as to be
> always valuable.
>
> *Thomas Jefferson*

Maes-y-Neuadd has been designated by the government as a building of
both architectural and historic interest. People first lived within some of
its walls in the fourteenth century. Three centuries later it was Oliver
Cromwell's headquarters during a Welsh campaign, and the name of the
Cromwell Bar commemorates those times.

    Some rooms are furnished with antiques, greetings are warm, and the
atmosphere is peaceful. Cooking is good, with vegetables picked from
the hotel's own gardens. We enjoyed a delicious afternoon tea on a
terrace in the sun. From the hilltop setting, we gazed across fields and

over treetops to sparkling Cardigan Bay, admiring the same glorious views that had been familiar to Cromwell and his Roundheads.

Mount Snowdon, highest mountain in England or Wales, where the first successful Mount Everest team trained, is only 13 miles away. You won't need to climb to get to its top. The only mountain rack railway in the British Isles will take you to the summit to see some of the grandest scenery in Britain. On clear days, the Wicklow hills in Ireland and the Isle of Man are visible.

Proprietors: June and Michael Slatter and Olive and Malcolm Horsfall. *Closed:* Three weeks in early January. *Recreational facilities:* Golf, tennis, riding, and swimming in ocean, lake, river, or indoor pool a short drive away. *Other facilities:* Lounge, cocktail bar, garden. *Rooms:* 12 with bath and TV. Breaks. No children under 7. Moderate. *Restaurant service:* Snacks, tea, dinner. *Credit cards:* Amex, Master, Visa. *How to get there:* Maes-y-Neuadd (pronounced Mice-er-Nayath) is signposted on Route B4573 between Harlech and Portmadoc and is about half a mile off the road. *Telephone:* (0766) 780 200. [T]

INDEX OF INNS
(WITH POSTAL CODES & RATES)

Postal codes have been listed following the name of the inn. The prices listed in this index were those for two people in high season in 1984. Unless otherwise indicated, they included breakfast (usually a full breakfast but occasionally a Continental breakfast). Rates are given in pounds, with their dollar equivalents in parentheses. The dollar exchange rate was figured at $1.17 to the pound. Where two prices are given, they are for the lowest- and highest-priced double rooms. Many establishments offer lower prices off season. Always ask for the current rates before you make reservations.

The following abbreviations are used:

    EP = European Plan — no breakfast

    MAP = Modified American Plan — rates included dinner and breakfast

Angel Hotel (1P33 1LT), 56; rates: 51-62 (72-87) EP
Appletree Holme Farm (LA12 8EL), 36; rates: 52-68 (73-96) MAP
Arundell Arms (P116 0AA), 118; rates: 42-49 (59-69)
Aspen Hotel (AB3 5SB), 194; rates: 18-20 (26-28)
Aynsome Manor (LA11 6HH), 59; rates: 56-61 (79-85) MAP
Bailiffscourt Hotel (BN17 5RW), 67; rates: 75-95 (105-133)
Banchory Lodge (AB3 3H6), 197; rates: 64-70 (90-98)
Bay Tree (OX8 4LW), 54; rates: 39-57 (55-80)
Bear (OX7 1SZ), 186; rates: 82-103 (115-145) EP
Bell Inn (HP22 5HP), 29; rates: 63-90 (87-126)
Bibury Court (GL7 5NT), 32; rates: 36-40 (51-56)
Black Horse Inn (PE10 0LY), 100; rates: 48 (68)
Bontddu Hall (LL40 2SU), 233; rates: 52-61 (73-85)
Bootham Bar Hotel (YO1 2EN), 188; rates: 36 (51)
Boscundle Manor (PL25 3RL), 152; rates: 50 (70)
Broadway Hotel (WR12 7AA), 49; rates: 48-64 (68-90)
Browns' Hotel, 216; rates: 38 (54)
Bull Hotel (CO10 9JG), 131; rates: 48 (68)
Burghope Manor, 185; rates: 60 (84)
Bwlch-y-Fedwen (LL49 9RY), 245; rates: 48-51 (67-71) MAP
Cardney House, 206; rates: 46 (65) MAP
Carwinion (TR11 5JA), 137; rates: 50 (70)
Chewton Glen (BH25 6QS), 142; rates: 88-120 (124-168)
Clifton Hotel (IV12 4HW), 224; rates: 44-62 (62-87)
Close, The (GL8 8AG), 165; rates: 46-69 (65-97)
Collin House (WR12 7PB), 50; rates: 48-53 (68-75)
Combe House (EX14 0AD), 91; rates: 47-62 (66-87)
Connaught, The (WIY 6AL), 121; rates on request
Court, The, 89; rates: 39 (55) MAP
Crosby Lodge (CA6 YQ2), 77; rates: 53 (75)
Crown (BA5 2RP), 172; rates: 42-47 (59-66)
Culloden House Hotel (IV1 2NZ), 217; rates: 89-120 (125-168)
Dedham Vale Hotel (CO7 6HW), 79; rates: 55-70 (77-98)
Dryfesdale Hotel (DG11 2SF), 223; rates: 30-42 (42-59)

Tillmouth Park (TD12 4UU), 70; rates: 49-54 (69-76)
Treglos (PL28 8JH), 69; rates: 85-88 (119-124) MAP
Tregoose Old Mill (SW96), 153; rates: 26-35 (37-49)
Tudor Arms (TN18 5DA), 102; rates: 36-44 (51-62)
Tullich Lodge (AB3 5SB), 194; rates: 76-86 (107-121)
Uplands Hotel (IP15 5DX), 24; rates: 39-44 (55-62)
Wensleydale Heifer (DL8 4LS), 173; rates: 32-50 (45-70)
West Arms (LL20 7LD), 243; rates: 38-41 (54-58)
White Hart (LN1 3AR), 120; rates: 46-52 (65-73) EP
White Moss House (LA22 9SE), 95; rates: 98 (138) MAP
White Shutters (FK17 8BN), 200; rates: 15 (21)
Whitwell Hall (YO6 7JJ), 178; rates: 41-58 (58-82)
Wilbraham (SW1Y 9AE), 130; rates: 42-66 (59-93) EP
Wild Boar Hotel (LA23 3NF), 75; rates: 62 (87)
Willmead Farm (TQ13 9NP), 44; rates: 26 (37)
Winterbourne Hotel (PO38 IRQ), 41; rates: 61-69 (86-97)
Woodlands (BD24 0AX), 90; rates: 30 (42)
Worsley Arms (YO6 4LA), 109; rates: 56 (79)
Ye Olde Bell (SL6 5LX), 111; rates: 38-55 (54-77) EP
Ye Olde Masons Arms (EX12 3DJ), 47; rates: 40-60 (56-84)

Send us your name and address...
...and we'll send you a free gift.

If you purchased this book, we'd like your name and address for our mailing list. Just supply the information below, and we'll send you your free gift.

I purchased this book at:

☐ Atticus
☐ Barnes & Noble
☐ B. Dalton Booksellers
☐ Bookland
☐ Books Inc.
☐ Crown Books
☐ Encore Books
☐ Hunter's Books
☐ J.K. Gill

☐ Kroch's & Brentano's
☐ Lauriats
☐ Marshall Field & Co.
☐ Paperback Booksmith
☐ Readmore
☐ Stacy's
☐ Taylors
☐ Upstart Crow & Co.
☐ Waldenbooks

Other:_____ (City)_____

I purchased this book on (approximate date):_____

Please send my free gift to:

Name:_____

Street or Box:_____

City_____State_____Zip_____

Please mail to:
The Compleat Traveler, c/o Burt Franklin & Co., Inc.
235 East 44th St., New York, N.Y. 10017 U.S.A.

Limit: One per customer.   **Limited time offer.**

THE COMPLEAT TRAVELER'S READER REPORT

To: *The Compleat Traveler*
    c/o Burt Franklin & Co., Inc.
    235 East 44th Street
    New York, New York 10017 U.S.A.

Dear Compleat Traveler:

I have used your book in _____ (country or region).
I would like to offer the following ☐ new recommendation, ☐ comment,
☐ suggestion, ☐ criticism, ☐ or complaint about:

Name of Country Inn or Hotel:

_____

Address: _____

_____

Comments:

Day of my visit: _____ Length of stay: _____

From (name): _____

Address _____

_____ _____ Telephone: _____